Improve Your People Skills:

Build and Manage Relationships, Communicate Effectively, Understand Others, and Become the Ultimate People Person

By Patrick King, Social Interaction Specialist at www.PatrickKingConsulting.com

Table of Contents

Improve Your People Skills: *Build and Manage Relationships, Communicate Effectively, Understand Others, and Become the Ultimate People Person* 3
Table of Contents... 5
Introduction 7
Chapter 1. Take Ownership and Responsibility 13
Chapter 2. Find Secondary Self-Interests....... 23
Chapter 3. Reform Toxic Habits 35
Chapter 4. Question Your Assumptions......... 53
Chapter 5. On Listening with Intent............... 65
Chapter 6. Emotional Intelligence 81
Chapter 7. Open the Door! Belief Police! 93
Chapter 8. The Four Communication Styles 103
Chapter 9. Walk a Mile 125
Chapter 10. The Value of Shutting Up 145
Chapter 11. Connect Instantly 159
Chapter 12. Workplace Tactics 177
Conclusion 191
Speaking and Coaching 193
Cheat Sheet.. 195

Introduction

In my opinion, one of the greatest movies in existence is *Back to the Future*—specifically the first of the trilogy, though the third edition shouldn't be discounted. We can just forget the second movie ever happened, but I digress.

It's no secret among my friends that I love the movie, and that I have semi-serious aspirations to purchase a DeLorean someday. Disappointingly, this story is not about my fondness for all things 1980s.

A friend was hosting a dinner party that was a loosely veiled front for a matchmaking event—each friend had to bring a single friend of the opposite sex, and we were told to "dress to impress." This had the makings of a fun night—or so I thought.

All went well until I met Dorothy. She was pleasant at first, but when I happened to mention my love of *Back to the Future*, things turned sour. She made a face as if she had smelled a dirty diaper and proceeded to give me her opinion on *Back to the Future*, her theories on time travel, and every inconsequential plot hole in the movie.

Did you know that Michael J. Fox wasn't even the original actor cast for Marty McFly? He wasn't that great anyway.

Why didn't the characters just tell the truth to each other?

Why was Marty's mom attracted to her own son? It's so unrealistic. (As if the glaring plot hole for a movie on time travel was being attracted to Michael J. Fox.)

After her monologue on the movie, it was clear

her conclusion was that the movie was terrible, that I should feel bad for liking it, and that I was even a little bit terrible. Even after I tried to walk away from the conversation-turned-lecture, she cornered me by the pizza rolls later that night and tried to re-state her points and make sure I agreed.

I remember thinking at that point how she was one of the most annoying people I had ever met, but it wasn't until later that I was able to articulate why.

She was a full-blown, card-carrying member of the *Belief Police*. She was the person who would track you down just to tell you that you were wrong.

In these people's minds, it's unfathomable that people can have different beliefs and think differently from them. They can't stand the fact that you disagree with their perspective or come to a different conclusion, and they attempt to patrol your brain for disagreeable beliefs and thoughts.

These are the same people who will tell you that things based on your opinion or tastes are just plain wrong. They aren't malicious, but this behavior comes from a stunning lack of self-awareness.

Awareness, openness, and listening are all cornerstones of becoming the consummate people person—the person in the room who can handle any situation and always knows how to react. It may seem like an understated part of life, but in reality, it's the ability to get what you want, no matter what. We never deal and struggle with circumstances—we deal and struggle with *people*. *People* are the gatekeepers, not your resume or anything else you might assume is more important than how well you interact with others.

These are teachable concepts, and though you might not be a member of the Belief Police, it's often the smaller, more nuanced signals we send out that repel people, or make us less trustworthy and liked. You can call them interpersonal skills, people skills, or just how to get along with anyone. Whatever the label, they pave the path towards extraordinary relationships wherever you are.

I want to teach you the most important aspects of connecting with others and understanding them as a means to the action you want. Some of them seem counterintuitive, common sensical, or too nuanced to matter—but that's the thing; they do matter, and it's people's tendencies to completely ignore them that leads to an interrogation over pizza rolls. After all, if everything was obvious, you wouldn't be interested in this book, would you?

For the record, I didn't change my opinion on *Back to the Future*.

Chapter 1. Take Ownership and Responsibility

Traveling: the more you do it, the more you love it—or hate it, because of the realities of traveler's diarrhea and the jet lag that comes with shifting time zones.

Traveling means something different to all of us, but there is something we all have to get through—the planning phase. If you're traveling with a friend, this can cause you to act in one of two ways during that phase.

If you know they love to plan and have a GPS functioning inside their brains, you will probably relax and blindly follow them. You might feel free to kick your feet up and trust that they know what they are doing. You'll put all of the responsibility into their hands and focus your attention elsewhere.

On the other hand, if you know and are aware that your friend is rubbish with a map and can't navigate his way out of a paper bag, you might approach your trip far differently.

What's the difference in these two approaches? You'd either take ownership or not.

If you know your friend is useless at planning, you would take it upon yourself to be accountable for what happens during the trip because no one else would. You'd approach the trip far differently, and check every box required to make sure it went smoothly. Just knowing that you if you don't do anything things won't get done will make you mentally dig in for the long haul in a very different way.

Here's another example of ownership in action.

Suppose two people move to a new city. One

decides to actively meet new people, and makes a point of being proactive about seeking out events to attend and activities to participate in. The other goes to work, and then goes straight home afterward, all the while wondering why he can't meet new people.

Clearly, one of these people in a new city will fare better than the other socially, and it's all due to the degree of responsibility and ownership they hold towards their own fate. If you think it's only up to you, chances are far greater that you'll do something about it, whatever *it* is. It's the same with your interpersonal and people skills. You can't assume that others are going to help you out and make interactions go smoothly or even comfortably. You can't even assume people are going to speak to you first and welcome you into their group of friends. This is your duty, and thus you must take ownership over it!

If you're failing, people won't bend over backwards to help you remedy a situation or solve a conflict for you. You need to accept sole responsibility for your interpersonal interactions. That is the first step toward improving them and becoming the people person you have inside of you.

When you take ownership, you'll think about your interactions beforehand, prepare for them, and proceed to bite your nails until you're sure they are good. This very natural level of anxiety combined with forethought is the secret and often-overlooked foundation of amazing skills in any aspect of life.

Most people have the tendency to blame others for their failures and shortcomings, and doing so exempts you from responsibility and thus the ability to look at your own actions honestly so that you can improve. In social and interpersonal terms, doing this causes you to make excuses and mutter things like, "Wow, they were so weird and boring and hard to talk to" or "What was wrong with them" instead of looking in the mirror at yourself and wondering what you could have done better.

If you walk through the day and can't find a single person to engage in friendly banter with, it's not because everyone is "unfriendly" or "awkward"—it's because *you* are.

The key to constant and consistent improvement of interpersonal skills is to hold yourself accountable for the process. This way, you put yourself in a position to constantly adjust, modify, and learn. Only a tiny fraction of the people you meet have excellent people and interpersonal skills. They weren't born that way. They may have been naturally gifted, but that doesn't mean they didn't capitalize on their strengths. Whatever the path, these individuals learned to deal with people on an incredibly high level to produce the positive outcomes they enjoy. They almost certainly took ownership of these skills to intentionally cultivate them because a skill won't grow on its own.

What does the opposite of taking ownership look like?

Hopefully, it doesn't sound too familiar:

instead of directly taking action on your life, you assume the role of a passive audience member and view your life from the sidelines. It's as if you're watching the movie of your life and there's really nothing you can do besides watch the scenes play out according to a script you didn't write. You're just stuck in your seat as things happen to you; you can't take action and make things happen. You are powerless and helpless. You are depending on external actions to occur *to* you, not taking action yourself. If you see a group of people talking, you don't engage them; you simply hope *they* break the ice with *you*.

Ultimately, it doesn't matter whether the other person is being cranky or whether the other person seems like they just have it out for you. You need to take ownership of creating a good relationship, interaction, or other interpersonal situation. What matters is how you choose to respond to the external stimuli life throws your way. If you approach them with a sense of ownership, your chances of producing positive outcomes increase tremendously. You put yourself in a position where you can take action to make things turn out for the better.

You have to make your own luck in the social realm; you cannot just sit back and hope you'll get lucky. One of your first steps might have been picking up this book. You may have realized that you can't rely on luck as a factor in your interpersonal success, so you are proactively looking for methods to increase the likelihood of social success.

The subtext under this entire chapter and even book is that you have to be the one to manufacture social interactions where you can make use of your people skills. Unless you realize your responsibility in (1) improving your people skills to be able to create those situations and (2) actually creating the situations themselves, you might continuously hit a wall and never move forward.

The added bonus of realizing you need to take ownership of situations is that you will prepare for all the contingencies you would not have thought about if you were placing responsibility on other people. You'll develop the habit of paying attention to small details and nuances in your interpersonal interactions that will allow you to be more interesting and charming. Just like with planning a trip, you'll obsess over where to stay and what to do each day just so you will feel prepared and comfortable.

Socially, you'll think *What if they say this, what if they do that, what if I sneeze and spill my drink all over them?*

Whatever you turn your attention to will grow in your mind and improve. With enough thought, we can often predict the direction a conversation or interaction will take. Being at least somewhat familiar with the possibilities and being prepared for them can be transformative.

Suppose you are on a rowboat with a man who only has one arm. Who might you expect to do the rowing? Don't just expect the other side to pick up the slack. You can't expect the world to open the door for you. You have to open it yourself, and you have to proactively step through it. Pretend that everyone you speak to only has one arm in the interaction. Don't expect any help and you'll be prepared when you don't receive any, and happily surprised and grateful when you do.

The bottom line is you have to take control over the *whole* process. Nobody's going to do it for you. Pretend that there is an invisible gas tank that represents each social interaction you have. You are responsible for filling 100% of it. Resolve to start behaving differently tomorrow compared to the unintentionally lazy template you're currently working with because obviously that template is not giving you the kind of results you want.

This book spells out the process by which you can take your people skills to the next level. However, in order for the tips in this book to be valuable to you, you have to start with the most basic—*you have to take ownership for them and use them.*

Think of taking ownership over your people

skills as acting like a hammer. What does a hammer see? Only things that need to be hit with a hammer.

Chapter 2. Find Secondary Self-Interests

Getting along better with people doesn't necessarily mean that you are making a new best friend every day. Getting along better with people on a realistic level mostly means that you *appear* to understand them on a deeper level; that you "get" them and their motivations—even if you don't. If you aren't able to achieve this level of understanding, you'll probably get more cold reactions than warm ones.

For instance, this is why we play the "Where are you from?" game and the "Oh! I spent some time there. Do you happen to know someone named Joe Johnson?" game when we first meet someone. We are innately seeking ways to imply understanding of each other, as it is the fast track to rapport and getting along. We want to show right off the bat that we are on the same page, and even think the same way.

This chapter is about finding a devastatingly simple way to understand people better right off the bat. There isn't a secret trick to making people feel that you "get" them; you just need to step into their shoes and view them as the same type of complex creature that you are yourself.

What do you care about? *Yourself and things that benefit you.* Now take a split second to think about their self-interests, and how they stand to benefit by an action, event, or statement. This is how you can immediately appear to understand people—by understanding what they are motivated by and generally want from any situation. You can think of this in the broadest of terms, and you can also drill down to tiny, specific interests.

Human beings are motivated by self-interest, whether we want to admit it or not. A lot of us talk a big game regarding altruism, but deep down we have a fairly narrow range of self-interests. If you are completely honest with yourself, you will see that a lot of the seemingly altruistic stuff you do is actually selfish to some degree.

That's not necessarily a negative, though. Without self-interest, the world would be an unpredictable mess. With it, people become much more predictable and act in patterns. Self-interest allows you to read this book—someone designed the computer or e-reader tablet out of self-interest, and Amazon sells products out of self-interest—even though others benefit. The world runs on self-interest, and understanding this will help you become the ultimate people person.

<u>Think Win-Win</u>

Now that you have a clear idea of the

importance of self-interest, the next step is to let it inform your social interactions. When you approach people in social situations, actively think about creating a win-win situation for both of your self-interests, or at least by knowing and acknowledging theirs.

You can also think of it in the following way: *you* win because you've satisfied your purpose in speaking and connecting with them; *they* win because you paid attention to their interests and added value to them. Even if you're not asking for anything, you will simply get more of what you want because you will address what's important to them and will have given them what they are looking for.

For example, if you approach a stranger at a networking event, a good strategy is to (1) determine their self-interest, and (2) deliver a win-win interaction by literally asking what they want to get out of the event.

Very often, they want to make high-level contacts or secure new business. Supposing this is the case, you could help them brainstorm about whom to meet and contact, and then you could help by introducing them around or engaging others in group small talk. You gain a new friend and ally, and they see their wallet swell. Here, you are acting as their wingman or even social lubricant to help them accomplish their goals. What's in it for you? You win by them considering you a valuable ally.

Other self-interests in a social setting are not related to goals at all: connecting with someone, meeting a good listener, feeling validated, making someone laugh, sharing about themselves—these are the real daily self-interests that you can help people achieve. Whatever the self-interest, make it known that you want to help others with it and you will learn quite a bit from how they respond to you.

When it comes to more structured settings such as the workplace, self-interests become even more important because you will constantly run into either conflict or a situation where one person wins at the expense of others. There's a reason things like office politics and workplace drama exist—because most everyone has the same intent and self-interest. In other words, there usually isn't enough figurative pie for everyone to eat their fill, and that creates bitterness or a clear win-lose situation.

An example of this would be where you and a coworker are both attempting to look good in front of your boss. The best way to look good in front of a supervisor is to engage with them, or work in a way that they can see your diligence. Obviously, there is limited face time available, so knowing your coworker's self-interest, you might help them look good in front of the boss in person, while you focus on sending diligent research and follow-up emails to show your worth. This is the same pie of your boss's attention, but you are feasting on the crust while allowing your coworker to feast on the strawberry filling. You can create a win-win situation by strategically allowing people to feel that they can reach their self-interest.

Secondary Self-Interests

Now suppose your coworker is exceedingly greedy and wants to block you at every turn. How can you make this into a win-win situation that doesn't feel as if you are just helping them sabotage you? This is where you start to look at people's *secondary self-interests*. This is where you truly to begin to understand people and their motivations.

That's the skill to develop and hone in this chapter. (1) If the primary pie is too small, what are the parts of the primary pie that people will enjoy? (2) What are the *secondary* pies that you can discover to keep all parties happy? Let's call these secondary self-interests, and they are what will really turn the tide in any interaction, whether friendly or adversarial.

So besides the promotion at work, what else motivates your coworker? In other words, what besides securing that promotion will make them happy and how can you help them with that? This is when you create another pie that only your coworker wants, so they can eat their fill without disturbing your self-interest. And even better, both sides still win.

Here, when you look to create win-win situations, you are looking to find other pies or give people the slice of pie they will most enjoy. Normally, when people compete, they always look to split a pie of resources in such a way that their slice is bigger and others have to lose out.

This is another layer of analysis you can start developing for yourself—what are the other person's less-mentioned motivating factors? What else do they desire in this context, and what would make them happy? There will always be more than one goal or objective.

In the case of your coworker, what else drives them to be so aggressive in demanding your supervisor's time?

Is it a need for validation and recognition, insecurity, a crush on the boss, feeling alienated in the office, not having office friends, a lack of awareness, and an assumption that you don't like them? Most of those are things you can easily address to satisfy their self-interest, which will naturally make them like you more and result in your getting along better.

People hate to lose or not get what they want. This is why too many people have a win-lose mindset. If you dig deep enough, you can find a way for them to feel as if they're winning with you, or better yet, *because* of you.

If you can properly identify and add value to others' primary and secondary self-interests, you can increase your people skills and how people perceive you. In many cases, that might be your only win, but it is a cumulative one with great cache.

The best part about this people tactic is that you can be fairly transparent about what you're trying to accomplish—helping their self-interests.

It's like when you are evaluating taking a new job. The primary self-interest might obviously be money and prestige, but those aren't the only things that matter for a new job. You are never making a decision in a vacuum, and that's where secondary interests come into play. *They might be secondary on paper, but they can often take precedence over primary interests.* This is because secondary interests tend to be more emotional and sentimental in nature. Think about the reasons you want to keep an old shirt—is it because you might actually wear it someday, or because it represents a memory of an old relationship from your hazy youth?

Or for example, with a new job, a shorter commute, a greater sense of community, an interesting work culture, working with people directly, or the great location might be more important than simple salary.

It should rarely be the case where you both reach for the same slice of pie. And with the knowledge of this chapter, it should never happen again. We are driven to be selfish through evolution, and it's what has kept us alive for all these years. It is one of the most stable predictors of human behavior, and you can apply this on a daily basis to the people around you. It's almost like reading people's minds, when in reality you just have to think about the plausible explanations for why people are engaging in certain behaviors. Go beyond the most obvious reasons and you'll instantly understand why people act the way they do.

Chapter 3. Reform Toxic Habits

One of my best friends never knows when to shut up.

Most of the time I enjoy this about him because he usually has something insightful or hilarious to say. He is forever a source of entertainment because he has no reservations about poking fun at every aspect of himself. He might be the most shameless person I know, and when he's around, you are sure to be either laughing or grimacing in a good way. His nickname in school was *the post office* because his mouth always delivered.

He isn't, however, a great listener.

This is showcased even in small instances, like when I want to rant about something inane that happened during my day, such as a driver cutting me off, or the market running out of my favorite kind of donuts (maple glazed) before I could get there.

The only purpose for those rants is to burn off some of my annoyance so it doesn't affect the rest of my day. It doesn't take long, and I'm not screaming or pounding the table. Really, all a person has to do to make me feel better is sit there, look pretty, and nod their head. No words are necessary, and I'm just looking for any type of actual understanding, even.

Despite all this, he just *has* to interject immediately and try to solve the problem or relate to an experience he had that was similar. For example, if I am indeed complaining about the absence of donuts, he'll immediately ask me what I can do about it, and suggest five actions for me to take to find the donuts from either their source, or petition the market to fry more in the afternoons. *Thanks, I wanted to discover how to become obese.*

I appreciate the gesture, but it's downright annoying when I can't finish my thought without hearing suggestions that I will never use and barely care about. Sometimes you just want to gripe a little and be heard; you are not actually looking for advice or even a solution.

This is what I would call a toxic habit. He's not toxic, but his habit of refusing to simply listen can be. It doesn't quite reach the point where I don't spend time with him or avoid him, but I do avoid him at *certain times* because of this. Despite how great a person you might be, you probably have toxic habits that repel people instead of attract them, and really, make you an anti-people person.

If "just be yourself" hasn't been working for you, then perhaps it's because "yourself" is grating, lacks tact, and doesn't play well with others. You just might have some habits that are blocking your path to being the people person you want to be. There's always room for improvement, and you have to be open to letting go of some key traits that you think make up who you are. Indeed, sometimes it's more important to fix flaws than to actually do something positive.

Bad Habit #1: You are never fully present

When you're talking with other people, you give out the impression that you'd rather be somewhere else, with someone else.

You think in the back of your mind that other people simply are not that interesting. To put it bluntly, you think most other people are boring. You expect others to entertain you and show disinterest, which doesn't even allow them to show their interesting sides. You expect people to be like a movie—to captivate you. It's bad enough that you think these things, but then you make it worse by telegraphing your feelings through your body language and your use of eye contact.

When people look at you, they can easily tell that you are not interested and in turn will think you not a nice person to be around. At best, you make people feel you simply don't care about them. At worst, you can come off as somebody who's flat out hostile.

And you know what? It's your fault for not valuing the person in front of you enough to make an effort. You're indulging your desire to search for something bigger or better.

Quick Fix

The quick fix to this bad habit is to admit that this is your fault.

If you think you're having a boring conversation that you want to get away from, you have to admit that you caused the problem. You caused the conversation to be boring because you expected it to be interesting, and you expected to be entertained by the other person instead of creating a conversation together.

How much work did you want to put in? You had a sense of entitlement, and because of your disengagement, the other person also got nothing out of the interaction. A conversation is two people, which means the burden should be equally split.

The fix here is to realize, appreciate, and understand that it's your job to make the conversation interesting. It's your responsibility; remember the chapter on ownership? Pretend that you are a talk show host and ask questions about them to figure out why they do the things they do. Ask questions about the opinions they hold. Make it your goal to find common ground or an interesting tidbit about their life.

This is only possible if you have a sense of curiosity about other people. And if you don't have a natural sense of curiosity about what goes on in other people's lives, fake it. Think of people you've wanted to meet since forever. What kind of questions would you ask them? Let people become aware of your sense of curiosity and energy and they will reciprocate.

Bad Habit #2: Your world is black and white

Put another way, you only see one correct way of doing things, and anything that diverges from that view is wrong. And that way happens to be your view.

This habit is particularly toxic because people who have this mindset are very judgmental. When they come across people who don't fit the mold of how they feel the world should operate, they judge them, sometimes to their faces. They are prone to thinking of that person as someone who is wrong, and can only respond in a very stereotypical way.

Just as you wouldn't want to be put in a box the moment you talk to people, they also don't respond all that well to feeling as if they're being judged. This is a hard habit to break because opinions can easily become personal. When you act this way, you tend to offend people and make them feel like they can't express themselves around you. Eventually, they'll just avoid you so they can avoid the feeling of having to censor themselves.

Unfortunately, our natural selfishness tends to translate to a black-and-white view in such a way that when our opinions are questioned, we ourselves feel judged and attacked. So people stop opening up to you, and will eventually avoid you altogether.

If somebody has an opinion, respect that opinion. Ask questions about how they came up with that opinion, and what information and assumptions they hold.

Quick Fix

This black-and-white thinking is actually very easy to solve. The vast majority of judgment comes from viewing yourself as superior to others. Therefore, the best way to undermine this toxic mindset is to consider alternative explanations to our judgmental statements.

Your grand explanation for something is just one possible conclusion that is neither better nor worse, just based on the information you have at your fingertips. Jog your creative faculties and try to understand how other people might have ended up with such a different opinion. Is their world view dramatically different from yours? What experiences have they had in their lives that might explain why they hold a position in such contrast to yours? Remember that people have their own reasons for opinions and beliefs and that not everybody thinks just the way you do. You can either recognize this or not.

Allow yourself to be curious as to how they reached their conclusion. Get excited about the story behind everyone and everything. Also recognize that judgment often comes from insecurity, jealousy, or resentment. Above all else, avoid making definitive negative statements in favor of ambiguous or curious statements.

Bad Habit #3: You are a conversational narcissist and dominate conversations

Some people are just in love with the sound of their voices.

They don't listen; they simply wait until the

other person stops talking so they can start speaking again. They view the time during which another person is talking as a resting period for their vocal cords. Their entire conception of a conversation is irregular—it's for them to talk about themselves and unleash the wealth of ideas from their brain into the world.

They don't acknowledge what others say. They don't even ask how the other person is doing. When people talk this way, it's because they find themselves more fascinating than the other people around them. It is extremely selfish and shows a deep and profound lack of interest in what drives, motivates, and interests other people.

Don't be the person who takes others hostage by talking their ears off. Again, eventually people will start avoiding you so their ears don't fall off.

Quick Fix

Thankfully, there is a quick fix to this

narcissistic conversational mindset.

Impose a limit on yourself. For example, for every story you share, you must ask the other person two questions about the story, or about things that are important to them. Keep track internally of how self-centered you are with regards to the topics you choose to talk about.

Challenge yourself to make your conversation a game to find out as much about other people as you can while saying as little as possible about yourself or the things you find interesting. Realize that people only feel good about and enjoy a conversation when they are sharing—you feel the same way. Allow others to feel good by giving them time and space to talk about what's important to them. Otherwise, people will start avoiding you because they will think of you as someone who doesn't care. They might already have started to.

This narcissistic conversational habit comes from a place of insecurity and a need to prove oneself. It can get boring quite quickly. Give others air space and know that the inclination to prove oneself immediately is a dead giveaway for insecurity. Impose a limit and even try to ask someone five questions in a row. If it's a hard task, then you'll know how much of a conversational narcissist you've been.

Bad Habit #4: You give unsolicited advice or opinions

This is my best friend to a tee.

Many times, people just want to talk about something and think out loud. They're not looking to debate, realize something profound, hear advice, or act on anything. They just want to be heard and validated in a comfortable setting. In many cases, they just want to get a weight off of their chest and share feelings. In fact, they want to hear their own voices. This doesn't mean they are conversational narcissists; they are simply having an internal monologue externally.

And that's it. That's all they're looking for. If

people want advice, they'll ask. After all, it's not like the solutions to people's problems are incredibly creative and require ingenuity. People almost always know what they need to do to solve their problem, they just don't want to hear it from others prematurely. They need to get to that point themselves, and a big part of the process is ranting and raving and thinking out loud.

You must be able to read people so you don't immediately turn them off by ignoring these central facts. When you give a response they were not looking for, people will begin to stay away from you.

Quick Fix

Take a moment to ascertain the purpose of a person's statement. Make it a binary choice: does this person actually want my input, or are they just letting off steam and need an ear to scream into? There is a big difference between the two.

If someone is asking for advice, let them ask

specifically and explicitly. Otherwise, shut up. If they don't ask you for specific advice or specific solutions, be content with being a simple sounding board. Just shut up.

You are either a sounding board or an advice columnist. It's not too hard to tell which, because people will either prompt you for more or continue speaking themselves. Allow people to spill their guts to you and they'll begin to trust you with other things as well.

Bad Habit #5: You always need to be right

There's an old saying, "I'd rather be happy than be right." (Probably made by a man in reference to marriage. Just kidding.)

Unfortunately, a lot of people prefer the opposite—to be right. They feel that they're coming off as weak if they give in. People like this always create excuses and rationalizations if anyone seeks to invalidate any part of their arguments or statements. They pick things apart that really don't matter just so they can stroke their own ego and be hold a sliver of moral and intellectual superiority.

They have a stunning lack of vulnerability, and it's extremely infuriating to speak with somebody with this mindset. It should be easy to see why. If you don't see it, you just might be this person. What lies beneath this façade is an interesting core of insecurity, in the sense that they feel they must prove their intelligence or else people will find them to be of no value otherwise.

This person doesn't make you feel as if you're having a dialogue. Everything turns into a black-or-white debate or argument.

Every interaction has to produce a winner and a loser. These people tend not to divulge anything personal or reveal any shortcomings because they feel doing so would undermine their perceived self, and because they are driven by extreme insecurity. They want to be seen as strong, and one way they feel they can make this happen is to be infallibly correct.

Quick Fix

First, you need to be aware that you're doing this.

Second, you need to be aware of why you're doing it. People who engage in this behavior are extremely insecure. They do this because they're trying to protect their ego and pride. They can't bear others seeing them as less than perfect.

There is no such thing as a perfect person. Trying to pretend that you are only makes you look ridiculous.

Third, learn to choose your battles. You can't simply blow up on every little argument you have with your friends. People will not take you seriously; remember the boy who cried wolf one too many times. If you feel the need to correct something, ask yourself if it actually matters or if it will come up again in any meaningful way. If the answer to those questions is no, then *let it be*. Letting it be is a difficult thing at first, but you'll find it to be a source of tension release after you grow used to not arguing about everything.

It's also important you realize that your perception is *your* reality. It's your fault if you're feeling attacked and judged all the time to the extent that you have to defend yourself. If this is the case, change your perception. There's no need for the unnecessary drama and negative fallout from your need to constantly be right.

When we think of habits, we typically think of bad ones such as biting your nails or picking your nose. It's really no different when it comes to social habits. People might love you, but if you embody one toxic habit, nothing else will matter. It's like saying, "If only that dog wasn't murderous, he's so cute and funny otherwise!"

Chapter 4. Question Your Assumptions

This is a story I've told many times because I find that it excellently illustrates the assumptions in our lives and why we should question them constantly.

I was assigned a parking spot at a new job, and in my second week, someone was parking in it every morning. I tried arriving earlier and earlier in the day to catch the culprit red-handed, but it took another couple of weeks because it seemed that this person woke up at the crack of dawn just to steal my spot.

What kind of sick person would do this

intentionally? They must have been a real demon, bitter at the world, or have held a huge grudge against me. Therefore, accordingly, I hated them as well. It consumed me for a few hours each day at work.

I was fuming about this the whole time, and when I finally decided to get there at 5:00 AM one morning, I found the culprit.

It was the company custodian who barely understood my greeting of "Hi, good morning, how are you?" He just nodded his head, grabbed his mop, and headed inside. It was clear to me that the whole notion of assigned parking spots would be lost on him, so I just went back to my car and napped until work started.

I was driven by the faulty assumption that whoever was parking in my spot was doing so maliciously. What was my assumption based on? No evidence of any kind, just a stab in the dark about intention. I should have questioned my assumptions before wasting hours of sleeping time to confront a kindly old man.

The way people behave is driven primarily by their assumptions and beliefs. So where do those assumptions and beliefs come from? It's not always clear, and sometimes they come from nowhere at all. But it's important to be aware of what you assume when you interact with people.

For example, if someone is quiet and sitting in the corner, what assumptions would you make about them? Maybe they're shy, introverted, and socially awkward? Not exploring alternative possibilities to your assumptions and not giving people the benefit of the doubt will cause you to act in a way that makes them indeed socially awkward. There are any number of reasons this person is sitting in the corner, and you pre-judging them closes doors immediately, no matter if you're right or wrong.

One of the biggest reasons people's interpersonal skills suffer is because of this exact process. People will make split second judgments and assumptions about others from tiny actions and never think twice about how incorrect the basis for their conclusions might be.

They'll put you in a position to be misunderstood and misinterpreted, without your even knowing it. If you make an incorrect assumption about someone, it will begin a cycle where both of you are communicating through subtext and passive aggressiveness.

The best way to face this is to remember that the majority of people possess a degree of *reasonableness*. Reasonableness is the opposite of intentional spite, or the sentiment that people are just out to get you in one way or another. There's a reason people are behaving in a certain way, it's not related to you, and it's not necessarily negative.

If reasonableness is your starting point, you'll have far fewer arguments. If you assume that people base their arguments and form their opinions based on logic, then it follows that they must be relying on facts and information you are not aware of. Most importantly, if you assume people don't hold any malice toward you, you are bound to view them in a more positive light.

If you make assumptions that ignore or undermine their logical flow and information, you are more likely to engage in meaningless arguments where one of the parties eventually exclaims, "Wait... *that's* what you thought I meant?" At the very least, you'll be stuck in your worldview and be continually surprised when people think differently from you.

There are a few assumptions that are particularly harmful when left unchecked, and can have a profoundly negative impact on your social interactions. It's okay to labor under these assumptions, as long as you can also provide alternative explanations for the conclusions you have arrived at.

Faulty Assumption #1: All parties understand what is being talked about

Are you even talking about the same thing? Or is there a fundamental disconnect that explains why there are such differences of opinion? Is there unnecessary confusion that has led to tension or conflict? Don't be afraid to stop completely and make sure everyone is on the same page. Too often people are so focused speaking at each other that they don't come to a mutual understanding.

Faulty Assumption #2: We already know the other person's view and opinions of the situation

Often, we think we know where someone is coming from and why they think that way. We are essentially filling in the blanks on how someone came to a particular conclusion or action. But how can you ever hope to be accurate? Unless you explicitly ask, there's no way to know for certain how someone feels about something, and the reasoning that led them there. We lack the ability to read other people's minds, yet we can sometimes be so convinced about why someone is trying to insult or damage us. Ask for other people's views and opinions and don't interrupt them.

Faulty Assumption #3: We are right and they are wrong

When you come to a situation with this assumption, there's no way it's going to end well or peacefully. This position on your part is the very opposite of giving someone the benefit of the doubt. You are completely invalidating their position and line of reasoning right off the bat and assuming moral and mental superiority. You go on the offensive and give them no choice but to assume the defensive.

Of course, it's a faulty assumption that you are correct in a certain circumstance. But if you know deep down that you are, or can prove it directly with evidence, at the very least, you don't have to be obnoxious and tactless about it. A better assumption to replace this is that you have your merits, but so do others.

Faulty Assumption #4: Everyone has the same set of facts

This is similar to Faulty Assumption #1, except

it assumes that if everyone were to have all the facts, the same conclusion would be drawn by all. It's an assumption that everyone has the same logic and makes the same mental leaps you do. Perhaps, yes, if everyone had access to the same set of information or background as you do, they would come to the same conclusion. Others just might be missing the key factors that make your argument *your argument*.

But information and learning is not equal, and it's rare that you overlap exactly with someone else's knowledge. This is naturally going to lead to misunderstandings and conflict.

Do you have any of these quick assumptions? When you believe these, you put people into boxes and make interactions more tense or adversarial than they need to be. You spit in the face of reasonableness and make it so people are either stupid, unreasonable, or backwards.

The better approach is to focus more on being curious and interested in what the other person knows and what facts have led them to their conclusion. This way, the conversation is not reduced to a simple matter of black and white. Instead, you open yourself up to learning new facts that might change your opinion or strengthen your opinion of the other person. Clearly, you can see how this might contribute to your people skills.

Here are a few more assumptions that have a bigger impact than you might realize.

Assuming impact is the same as intent

This is a particularly toxic assumption because you equate the bad effects of something with the intention of the person behind that action.

This is how I felt about the company custodian who kept stealing my parking spot.

Just because somebody did something bad does not necessarily mean that was their intent. In fact, with everything else being equal, this is almost never true. Unless you have solid facts to lead you to believe they intended the negative impact of their actions, jumping to that conclusion on your part will cause unnecessary animosity. Don't automatically conflate negative events with negative intentions or motives. Accidents truly happen and don't mean anything about people's motivations or intentions towards you.

Assuming that you are as subtle or as obvious as you think

Just because you think something is subtle doesn't necessarily mean the person you're speaking with sees it the same way. You cannot assume that people understand your quirks and mannerisms.

Only people who have known you for a long time or who have observed you in a wide range of circumstances will be able to get into your head and accurately interpret you this way. Most of the time this will not be the case.

We only share "I was thinking that too!" moments with a few people, so when you assume that people will be able to pick up on your subtleties or your obvious statements, you are assuming too much. Don't give other people the responsibility of essentially reading your mind because they'll almost certainly read it incorrectly.

You simply cannot assume that people understand your secondary or even primary meanings. This is especially true when it comes to jokes, where it's easy to come across in the worst way possible. This is when you'll hear people exclaim things like, "*OF COURSE I didn't mean it like that! How could I?*"

In many cases, you have to spell it out or do a better job of letting people know that you are joking.

Assuming that matters are personal

Just because something negative was said or proposed doesn't mean that it's a slight against you, or that there is a negative judgment about you. Often, these things are just observatory and people have much better things to do than fixate on your personal flaws. You can be a smart person and do something witless. It doesn't make you any less smart.

You can begin to embody a victim mentality when you feel that everything is a personal affront. Then it becomes a self-fulfilling prophecy because others will start to avoid you and become frustrated with you—then you truly are the one suffering.

It's almost never personal and learning not to react with emotion is key here.

Learn to quell this handful of damaging assumptions and your people skills will increase dramatically. The previous chapter discussed toxic habits—assumptions should be looked at as another type of toxicity that will repel people.

Chapter 5. On Listening with Intent

As a general rule of thumb, I tend to listen far more than I speak. I do this because I enjoy listening to people's stories, but more importantly, I like to give others *air space* in a conversation. Air space is simply the room to speak without feeling like they are going to be cut off, interrupted, or not share what they wish to share. I find people speak more freely and eagerly when they are given air space.

In some order, here's what people enjoy about conversations: being entertained, speaking and sharing, laughing, and learning something new.

Notice a pattern? If we aren't listening to something we feel has value to us, then we prefer to share about our lives and thoughts. Think about how you feel after you leave a conversation where you don't share much, and the air space was monopolized by the other person.

Your neck probably hurt from all that nodding and you felt as if you just left a lecture. You felt neglected. Now imagine a scenario where you were given all the air space you could possibly use and appeared to have a captive audience. You'll come away feeling much different, and that's the type of feeling you should attempt to impart to others by listening with intent.

To become a people person, you need to listen way more than you speak. The sad truth is that it's impossible that everything out of your mouth is going to be fascinating and compelling, so let others share—they'll feel better about themselves and subsequently about you.

There's a giant caveat—to be a good listener,

you aren't just giving air space and surrendering your turn to speak. A lot of people think that to be a good listener, you just need to shut up and let the other person talk. While to some extent that's true, there are more parts to the puzzle. That's passive listening. To the other person, it can feel as if they are speaking to a wall.

Active listening is the key to giving others validation. It reads like a mouthful, but it's simple in practice. You are listening with intent.

Let's say that someone says, "Last weekend I was skiing but I wasn't really having a good time." Passive listening would consist of you saying "Oh, cool" or "Uh huh" and only acknowledging their statement and staying silent afterward.

Active listening, and listening with intent, would consist of any of the following:

"Didn't have a good time...?" (Repeating the last phrase of a person's statement) or

"So you went skiing but it wasn't the best time?" (Rephrasing their statement back to them) or

"Sounds like you were expecting a fun and active weekend but something was wrong or missing?" (Sum up their thoughts and position)

When you read it from the page, it sounds like you might come off like a parrot or a robot. *Active listening is just repeating what someone says? How does that help?*

It helps because people hear far more than simple repetition. They are hearing you use their own words in a new sentence, which gives the strong impression that you were listening intently. It appears that you are following their train of thought with interest. You want to make sure with crystal clarity that you understand them so you can delve deeper.

The best part of all this is the more you do this, the more they will continue to talk and take the conversation into deeper realms. You can literally mix the three types of phrases for an hour and observe in wonder as people pour their hearts out attempting to explain, justify, and elaborate.

The intent is to crack them open like a nut and learn as much about their inner thought process as possible. People want to feel that they matter. People want to feel that what they have to say is something of consequence—that's the ultimate power of validation. Sound curious and non-judgmental, as if to ask, "Did I get this right? Please correct me if I did not."

I wasn't sure whether or not I wanted to travel this summer.

Travel this summer?

Yeah, I was thinking about going to Greece but it might be too expensive.

You want to go to Greece minus the prices?

Yeah, I haven't traveled anywhere in the past

few years and I've seen so many great pictures of the Greek Islands.

Sounds like you need to get away despite the cost!

You could be right. I mean, people are only young once, right? I've always dreamed of traveling the world but work gets in the way.

So work has always gotten in the way?

This conversation could probably continue *ad nauseum*, but notice how all one party is doing is picking and choosing phrases to repeat so that the other party is beckoned to clarify and elaborate further?

It's no wonder that this is the exact technique that psychologists use during therapy sessions to allow people to discover themselves and articulate out loud their inner thoughts. A few well-placed questions in the form of active listening can really crack people open, as well as help them learn about themselves. If you're great at listening with intent, it's impossible for you to become a conversational narcissist.

In most cases, when people share or want to get stuff off their chest, they're looking for a sense of validation. They're not going to get these if you are just going to sit there with a blank expression on your face. Recall that good listening demands active focus and participation.

The most common kinds of emotions people are trying to elicit are excitement, shock, interest, or amusement. These are what you should validate people on. Keep these emotions in mind and make sure to reflect them back—it tells them their message is on point and well-received, and it encourages them to share more.

The truth is that listening more enables everything else we are trying to accomplish in this book. When you listen more, you hear feedback from others and how they truly respond to you. When you listen more, you understand people more deeply and what motivates them. When you listen more, you can see if you possess a toxic habit or two.

This skill enables you to get into their world, and all it takes is for you to resist the temptation of interjecting or interrupting.

In the quest to become a better people person, listening well is perhaps the most universal theme—not just according to me. Consider that the following titans of industry made it to the top of their fields not because of their inherent intellect, but because of how they were able to work with and lead people.

"Two monologues do not make a dialogue." - Jeff Daly

Jeff Daly is a prominent American architect who previously served as head of design of the Metropolitan Museum of Art in New York. What is this quote saying?

First, when you speak with someone, you must make sure that it's a two-way street. It's not a lecture, and it's not sermon. It's an interactive dialogue where two parties collaborate to create something together.

Second, when you speak with someone, make sure that you are actually listening and engaged, as opposed to ceding the floor and simply waiting for your turn to speak again without acknowledging them. Often, we get the sense that we are only speaking at each other instead of with. If you walk away from a conversation with nothing gained or lost, this is what you've been doing.

Conversations are best viewed as opportunities for learning. They can be opportunities for building bridges instead of each party attempting to show just how intelligent they are. For real dialogues to take place, you have to have an open mind regarding what you can take away from the other person as far as your own personal education is concerned.

Keep an open mind, develop a sense of curiosity, and most importantly, attempt to be less self-centered—this is how you create meaningful and healthy dialogues.

"You can make more friends in two months by becoming interested in other people than you can in two years by trying to get other people interested in you." - Dale Carnegie

Dale Carnegie was the author of the seminal book, *How to Win Friends and Influence People*. He was widely regarded as a pioneer of the self-development movement, and his legacy continues today. There's a reason many people call his works generic and common sense—he's the one who made them so.

What exactly does Carnegie mean here? It's not very easy to make friends if you're trying to impress others and paint a good picture of yourself for them. In fact, that's downright counterproductive to making friends. All you're doing is becoming the windbag who lacks self-awareness and whom no one is interested in. People don't care about you; they care about themselves.

Taking an interest in people and letting them speak and share about themselves is how people will be more inclined to become friends with you.

We like people who are interested in us and think we are amazing. We also enjoy speaking about ourselves—most people are their own favorite topic and we like to explain our unique sensibilities. Seize advantage of this very simple fact and become more interested and curious about others and give them an outlet. You'll find that if you barely speak during a conversation, the other person will walk away feeling as if they've had an amazing experience.

Showing intense interest is an everyday superpower that will open people up more than you might expect. When's the last time you asked someone five questions in a row?

"Many attempts to communicate are nullified by saying too much." - Robert Greenleaf

Robert Greenleaf was the founder of the Servant Leadership movement, which is a leadership philosophy and approach toward managing people.

Setting aside what you want in a conversation can be key to having a good one. In other words, focusing on the other person and what they want out of the interaction, and what they want to say, will lead to better communication. There are two sides and yours doesn't take precedence over theirs.

You listen, hear concerns, allow them to speak, and validate them. That's difficult if you monopolize communication and only talk about your interests. Not only does nothing get accomplished, but if it does, it doesn't get done well because you didn't receive any feedback from others.

Communication is all about give and take. If you hog the spotlight, you run the risk of being not only a boring communicator, but an annoying one. Take an opposite tactic. Try to say as little as possible and get other people to speak more.

"I don't like that man. I must get to know him better." - Abraham Lincoln

Abraham Lincoln was the 16th President of the United States of America and is famous for delivering the Gettysburg Address, abolishing slavery, presiding over the presidency during the Civil War, and ultimately being assassinated.

The reason we don't like people or some people tend to irritate us is because we simply don't know them all that well. What little we do know we take and magnify and amplify, creating a caricatured version of them in our heads that is in no way accurate to real life.

We take what we see in the first 30 seconds from someone, and if it's negative, we assume that's their character. We have no reason to give them the benefit of the doubt. We judge.

But everybody bleeds, they hurt, and everybody, deep down, has the same basic wants and needs. Somebody might come off as obnoxious to you, but if you give them the opportunity to create a three-dimensional identity for themselves, you might find aspects of them that you actually enjoy or admire—or at least defensible justification for why they are the way they are.

You won't merely label them as obnoxious—they still might be, but they'll be a good person that is occasionally obnoxious, as opposed to unquestioned vermin.

In many cases, people are not inherently bad or good. Our impressions are usually just reflections of our assumptions or attitudes. Give people the benefit of the doubt and talk to them with an open mind. Listen to discover.

"Wise men speak because they have something to say; fools, because they have to say something." - Plato

Plato was one of the most prominent Ancient Greek philosophers, along with his teacher Socrates and his student Aristotle.

This is a final remark on the importance of listening. Wise people spend their time listening, observing, and thinking about the matters before them. Consequently, when they speak, people listen, because what they have to say is usually measured and wise. They think twice as much as they speak because that's what necessarily goes into a wise statement.

Fools on the other hand spend their time not increasing their knowledge by speaking, interjecting, and interrupting. This is the best way to not understand people and appear uninformed at the same time. They speak first without taking anything into consideration.

Communication is best when informed and measured, and silence is not always a bad thing. When you are going to speak, try asking yourself the reason for it.

Is it because you have something to contribute, or just because you want to fill the air or hear your own voice? What is necessary to say, and what should be discarded in favor of hearing the other person?

Listening with intent makes it clear that

communication occurs when air space is allowed to exist. The alternative may not necessarily be hatred and repulsion, but you are going to miscommunicate and feud more often than not.

Chapter 6. Emotional Intelligence

Emotional intelligence has become somewhat of a buzzword the past few years, but most people don't quite know what it means.

Emotional intelligence is knowing and perceiving the emotions you feel and why you feel them. You are able to put a label on your emotional state and find its cause and effect. By extension, emotional intelligence is being able to read other people's emotions accurately and deduce the reasons for them.

When you start thinking, "Why did she say that?" and "What made him do that?" instead of immediately reacting, that's the beginning of your path to emotional intelligence. Why does any of this matter?

People with the skill of emotional intelligence are less judgmental and more empathetic because they understand other people's motivations and intentions and how that influences their emotions. In times of conflict, they can cut past emotional reactions and resist taking matters personally. In social situations, it means that people with high emotional intelligence can know exactly what to talk about and what excites or bores people.

High emotional intelligence is like being able to read someone's mind. How do you gain this everyday superpower and increase your emotional intelligence?

The first step is to actively make an effort to know yourself better.

It's next to impossible to understand other people's thought patterns if you can't see your own with clarity. What follows sounds impossible, but you need to start *thinking about how you think.*

What you're really doing is taking a step back and pausing whenever you experience a strong emotion. Close your eyes and try to trace what happened in the past hour or two that led you to feel that way. Are there any facts or experiences in the past that would explain why you feel a particular way about certain things and people in your life? What is currently casting a subconscious shadow over your mood?

You might be surprised by what you discover.

For example, if you're angry at 6:00 PM, start thinking about what you've done since 3:00 PM. You've driven home, had a snack, changed into your sweatpants, and watched a little bit of television.

When you visualize your drive home, though, suddenly you remember that you were cut off by somebody and that you were beeped at incessantly. This agitated you and you were still feeling the effects of that mood dampener hours later. This is a simplification of the process that begins to take place much more instantly.

The sad reality is that most people are not in tune with their feelings. Often, we are negatively affected by the emotional impact of things that have long since been irrelevant. Most people just react automatically without realizing why and without stopping to think what is happening internally. They fall into patterns that are sometimes negative, and sometimes destructive.

Why do some people overeat? It's not because they're just perpetually hungry. It's because they're using food as therapy without realizing that they aren't hungry, just upset. Knowing yourself is probably the hardest job in the world. It's easier for us to judge other people than to actually take a long and honest look at how we feel and how we think. But it's key to understanding the thought patterns that others engage in.

The second step is to observe your actions.

Rather than looking inward and attempting to label your emotions based on what you might hypothesize caused them, analyze how you are acting and label them that way.

In the former, you are looking to the past to try to deduce a cause. In the latter, you are looking at the present to see the manifestation of emotion. In a sense, you are working backwards from what you see, and creating at least one theory about what caused it.

Just as with other people, you can tell more about yourself by your actions than you can by what you say (or what you tell yourself).

As with the first step, this requires a degree of introspection. When you act uncharacteristically, take a step back and think about the kind of emotions that typically galvanize such reactions. For example, if I was somewhat cold and unresponsive to my friend, I would need to think about what happened between us that subconsciously annoyed me.

It might stem back to something as small as him never having his wallet when the bill comes.

Notice how you act when you experience certain emotions, and you'll begin to see certain patterns emerging. At this point, it's very easy to slip into judgment mode and start attaching labels to your behavior. If you are acting in a way you shouldn't be acting, it's easy to judge yourself as a bad person.

This is a mistake that will just lead to a slippery slope of negativity. Your main focus right now is simply to get a clear picture of what drives and motivates you. It's very hard to come up with an honest picture if you're constantly judging yourself. You simply want to discover what makes you happy or sad.

Once you have that, you can work on the following step.

The third step is to practice responding instead of reacting.

People with high emotional intelligence eventually come to the realization that they can control their emotional states. This is made possible by knowing the causes and addressing them at that moment.

It's not so much of a confrontation with other people; it's the self-talk that is "That's why I was upset. I felt insulted because Dave forgot to bring his wallet again for the fifth time in a row. It's not actually a big deal. I should have no problem going back to my normal mood now."

That's the meaning of *responding versus reacting*. Letting your emotions govern you means you are reacting instead of responding. Responding is crucial because it involves premeditation. You're taking all the factors into consideration and making an informed choice as to what to say and how to act. Reaction, on the other hand, is simply letting your emotions get the best of you. It's often unbalanced and in many cases leads to a negative interplay of emotions with others.

When you react negatively to somebody it provokes a negative response in turn, and you then respond even more negatively. It's a race to the bottom.

When you are don't know what you are feeling, you don't know how to react or make yourself feel better. But the act of simply putting a label on your emotions gives you a tried and true set of behaviors to get yourself back to your status quo. You know how to deal with anger, sadness, and annoyance. You *don't* know how to deal with a hazy feeling of negativity.

Knowing yourself must come first. If you're not self-aware, all your efforts at trying not to step on people's toes will fail. Your inability to get around your emotions will tint your reading of how other people feel.

Here is a short list of factors to help boost your emotional intelligence. Ask yourself these questions—one at a time at first, and shortly they will become instinctual habit. It's not an easy task because you can't focus on one factor definitively. Each situation is different, and you must be adaptable in discovering why people feel what they do. Going through this checklist will assist you in reading people's emotions in a way you may never have considered before.

- How might your thoughts and actions might be misinterpreted?
- What are other people's primary motivations and what unspoken, underlying motivations might they have that they (and you) are not even aware of?
- Consider people's built-in biases and life circumstances that give rise to certain emotions. What is their background and upbringing?
- How do people display their emotions both positively and negatively?
- How are emotions displayed in different ways?
- What is their baseline emotional state and preferred interaction style?

By being aware of these factors, you increase your emotional intelligence because you are able to read people more accurately. And just as important, you can respond to them in a more calibrated manner that leads to fewer negative reactions. Notably, this process can take a while—exactly the difference between responding and reacting.

At the most basic level, emotional intelligence is knowing the range of reactions to any given statement or circumstance, and who might respond differently and why.

If you insult someone's mother in a serious manner with a serious face, one reaction would be anger and being offended. You can expect that reaction a majority of the time. However, what are the other possible reactions, and what accounts for the difference? People might assume you are joking, laugh out of confusion, or ignore you because they didn't even hear what you said.

Emotional intelligence will allow you to connect with people on a deeper level because you understand them implicitly without their saying anything. You will just get them. This is what many people interpret as chemistry and rapport, and you will have it in a seemingly effortless manner.

Chapter 7. Open the Door! Belief Police!

Have you ever had that feeling that you just needed to set the record straight on something?

It might not even concern you, and it certainly doesn't affect your life. The other person also likely won't care that much. In cases like this, if you were to really think about it, it becomes fairly clear that we are only doing this for ourselves. There's absolutely nothing in it for either of you except for your feeling of feeling superior or not inferior.

That's all we're seeking when we seek to set

the record straight most of the time. Why is this such a compelling feeling? Because you can't stand the idea of someone believing something that you don't, especially if it makes you appear to be in the wrong.

In short, you are a full-fledged, card-carrying, badge-wearing member of the *Belief Police*.

This causes us to spend way too much time squabbling over things that really don't move the needle just because we feel that other people believe or think something different than we do and must be corrected. If we're honest, it's because our ego feels a little bit bruised so we feel the need to inflict that same feeling on others.

If you've ever been around a know-it-all, you know exactly what I'm talking about. If you don't, you might be a member of the Belief Police. *Open the door! You're wrong about something!*

Whomever you're speaking with, there will inevitably come a point where you don't match up with them. If it's about a topic that you have a personal investment in, it's easy to get in over your head and try to win the other person to your side. You think, "How could anyone think any differently? The conclusion is so clear!"

But how often does it actually matter beyond that very minute that you're thinking about it? The vast majority of the time, this kind of squabbling occurs in places like the comments section of a YouTube video or the comments section of a news blog. When you scroll down into the rabbit hole, you will see people arguing over the smallest pedantry and nitpicking for days. Mostly, the arguments are between two people who simply don't want to give any ground. Who knows how many of their waking hours they have been composing retorts to that nasty YouTube commenter?

We feel that since we know so much better than the other person, we have some sort of responsibility to correct them. In other cases, we know that we're right about something and the other person is wrong in a black-and-white sense. We then take it upon ourselves to prove to them just how smart we are. We just can't stand someone believing something wrong or contrary to what we believe!

These tendencies play out all the time, and in many cases, they involve issues that are of very little importance. You want to be right all the time—the Belief Police typically do.

A Belief Policeman might be very effective at imposing their beliefs on others, but this habit is going to make you downright obnoxious to talk to, and not in an affectionately obnoxious kid sister kind of way. People will avoid you. Who wants to spend time with someone who makes them feel judged, attacked, and defensive?

The bottom line is that the bulk of these arguments all stem from the all too human tendency to "police" other people's beliefs.

The underlying assumption is, "I have to show them I'm right and make them bow to my knowledge." Everything is a pissing match—

and as is always the case—borne out of supreme insecurity.

Everything is an opportunity to show just how vastly superior your knowledge and experience are compared to the person you are conversing with. Because otherwise, you'd be seen as inadequate and inferior, right? Instead of saying, "Well, you could be right. You might have a point. Moving on!" you stand your ground and want to show intellectual dominance. The great part about this type of statement is you're not making an actual assertion or conceding to their position; you're just validating them and moving on.

Yet...

You have to catch yourself when you slip into this mode because it is not only subtle, but also very addictive because of the payoff at the end. Let's face it; it feels amazing when someone acquiesces and says, "Yeah, you're right. I'm wrong."

But at what cost does this come? And in the

end, does it really matter?

If you took an aerial view of your heated conversations with your friends, coworkers, associates, and colleagues, in almost all cases you would probably conclude that almost none of it truly mattered. Your pride and ego did, but not the issue at hand.

Most of the time, the reason you have such arguments is that you have taken on the role of Belief Policeman. You've given yourself the job of patrolling other people's minds, assumptions, and beliefs.

Not only is it completely unnecessary, it is almost always unwelcome with small matters. What about intimate and personal matters, such as if you expressed your religious beliefs and someone couldn't stop trying to convert you to a different religion? What if you expressed your love of a certain food or drink and someone just couldn't stop telling you how disgusting they were?

What if you expressed your opinion on a

favorite movie or television show and someone couldn't stop telling you that you *needed* to watch other shows?

It's frustrating being the recipient of this attitude because you feel attacked, and it's not as if they are going to change your mind anyway. It's futile. So what gives you reason to think that it's not going to be unwelcome when you do it to other people? It says more about you than it does about them if you feel the need to constantly interject your opinions and thoughts. Being part of the Belief Police is for your benefit, not theirs, even though in your mind you are seeking to benefit them with your knowledge.

You're just stroking your ego and making sure people know your worth. Ironically, this makes people value you even less because it is one of the hallmarks of insecure and overcompensating behavior.

Follow this simple rule to break out of this behavior pattern: don't share your opinion unless asked. Unless someone has explicitly asked you for your opinion, or is quite obviously soliciting your arguments as part of a debate, don't engage them and try to let it slide. Err on the side of neutral.

Engage momentarily just to acknowledge that they do have an opinion and you might even throw in your opinion there, but don't attempt to convince or police them.

This is especially true when it comes to matters of taste and opinion. These are completely subjective. What looks good to you might be completely ugly to another person. You won't convince anyone to like chocolate more than they already do, or to like beets when they hate them, so, it's really a waste of your time—and an extremely annoying one at that—to exert your energy trying to convince them.

The bottom line is if something is not affecting you directly, or it's a one-time occurrence and the issue is something that is near and dear to your heart, choose to resist the temptation to be the Belief Police. In fact, resist the temptation more than that.

Just let others be right (or think they are right) most of the time. Choose your battles and don't fret about the small details of what you can't change. You'll be happier and less stressed, and you'll notice a direct correlation between that and the quality of your friendships and interactions.

Chapter 8. The Four Communication Styles

When I was still practicing law, it was no surprise that I would often come across aggressive personalities.

These were the types of people who wanted to dominate their opponents, whether in the courtroom, through documents, or in the cafeteria. They went to law school to try to be the best, and their goal-orientedness was occasionally admirable.

However, they are a large part of the reason I got out of the legal industry. I had a sense of dread when I would open emails from opposing counsel, and occasionally from my supervising partners. Meetings were never very pleasant, and I found myself often thinking, "Hey, why can't we all just relax a little bit?"

The reality was that I didn't know there were different communication styles, and what drove the people who adhere to each style. I could get along just fine with people who were relaxed—in other words, similar to me. But that wasn't going to help me very much when dealing with strangers and generally getting what I wanted.

One of the many keys to playing well with others, no matter who they are, is being able to identify their communication style and thus understand them better. This chapter is about understanding how they're different from you and understanding how these differences can be reflected in the ways they choose to communicate what they believe and what they think.

By using this style-based approach to friends

and strangers, you can create a framework with which to deal with people—and it might surprise you in how well it works. We can come up with a semi-predictable map on how to deal with certain types of people. In the same vein, by knowing how certain personality types tend to think, behave, and interact socially, we can also avoid unnecessary conflict and awkward moments.

For example, if I knew there were four main communication styles and that I was dealing with aggressive communication, I would know to speak in a way that furthered their goals and to avoid pleasantries and small talk. The currency of an aggressive communicator is progress toward their goals—and feeling that you can help them to those ends is how you can become likable to someone like that. People don't enter conversations, work or social, with the same intentions. You must understand and cater to that.

There are four main communication styles— attempt to discover which most describes you, and which most fits the people you spend the most time with. The four styles are passive, aggressive, passive-aggressive, and assertive.

Knowing someone's style can transform how you interact with them. Sometimes, it can be like a lightning bolt of clarity, not unlike when you stare at a pattern and suddenly the three-dimensional picture starts to form in your head out of the pattern.

Passive Communication

Passive communicators avoid expressing their opinions or feelings.

They avoid any type of conflict, and this involves standing their ground and even claiming their rightful privilege. None of that matters to them; they'd prefer that others draw attention to them instead of doing it themselves.

They often see their needs ignored. They are often categorized as wallflowers, and will communicate only as much as possible to get their message across one time. If there is a conflict, they may not speak up. Passive communicators tend to speak softly or apologetically. When passive people talk, they usually convey one of the following feelings:

- I won't stand up for myself or my rights.
- I don't know what my rights are and I don't care.
- I am okay being a doormat.
- I need the help of others to assert myself.
- No one, including me, considers my feelings.

You can see the common thread—passive communicators don't feel secure in their abilities or identity, and this fear keeps them silent and out of the spotlight. The best way to engage passive communicators is to approach them gently, make sure you don't use judgmental language, and encourage them by complimenting and emphasizing their worth.

They'll be reserved and guarded until they feel safe with you, and that's a process that can take some work and time.

Yes, you might feel like you need to coddle the passive communicator. It is low self-esteem that has left them interpersonally crippled. However, every team (or friend group) needs someone who skews this way because otherwise everyone would be butting heads all of the time. Accommodation needs to occur at some point.

Aggressive Communication

Aggressive communicators tend to be self-centered. It's not intentional, but they think more about themselves and thus tend to violate the space of others because they prioritize themselves.

It's not just confidence, but over-confidence, because it goes beyond personal boundaries and is driven by a need to dominate, conquer, and prove others wrong.

People with an aggressive communication style are always out to prove a point. It is not uncommon for aggressive communicators to be verbally abrasive. You would be right in expecting that they also react poorly when challenged or proved wrong.

Aggressive communication is typically the result of low self-esteem.

People who have an aggressive communication style might be suffering from unhealed emotional wounds and deep down feel powerless. Aggressive individuals display a low tolerance for frustration and tend to use humiliation and conversation interruption to try to assert themselves. In their minds, they're simply standing up for their rights, because they've made the mistake of not standing up for them before. You're right to think many of their behaviors are aimed to keeping their egos un-bruised and protected.

In a sense, it's the mindset of "I'll never be disrespected again," which causes them to disrespect others. Accordingly, they'll use whatever is available to them to stand up, often involving criticism or blaming or attacking others.

They tend to be goal-oriented around this, so they have a tendency not to be good listeners.

Aggressive communicators express statements that convey the following:

- The other person is inferior and wrong.
- The problem is all the other person's fault.
- I am superior and correct as a rule.
- I'm going to get my way regardless of the negative consequences.
- I am entitled to things and other people owe me.

Aggressive communicators are often uncomfortable with themselves, and they lash out at other people to alleviate that tension and make themselves feel better. A direct challenge to an aggressive communicator can escalate quickly into a pissing match where there will never be a winner.

Knowing that they are focused on protecting their perceived rights and getting what they feel is owed them, you should handle aggressive communicators as you would an angry child.

Validate them and let them know they have been heard. Placation, in other words, is the action prescription. Once they can see that you recognize their greatness, or are simply not a threat to their pride and ego, they will let you in. Aggressive communicators might seem like a pain to deal with, but the reality is we need these personality types as well. They are a great fit for my former progression of law because lawyers need to assert their clients' feelings of righteousness. You'll be glad this personality type exists when you have one on your side, instead of across from the table.

Passive-Aggressive Communication

Passive-aggressive communicators appear passive on the surface. And of course, deep down, they are acting passively with a purpose, and out of anger. They are like ducks—serene on the surface, but paddling furiously just below the water line.

Passive-aggressive communicators use

subtlety, misdirection, and contrived tests to communicate their message and attempt to get their way. Therefore, they may appear passive, but they are still trying to enact the approach of the aggressive communicator.

They want to assert dominance over people and a situation, but they want to do it in a way that lets them appear socially acceptable and polite. Direct confrontation is their worst nightmare—they'd rather manipulate their goals into reality. Think of the aggressive communicator as the male schoolyard bully, whereas the passive-aggressive communicator is female schoolyard bully who rules through psychological warfare. The aggressive communicator will confront a roommate about washing the dishes, whereas the passive-aggressive communicator will leave a note that reads, "Hi, can you please be more considerate and wash the dishes next time? Thanks!"

Passive-aggressive communication usually has an undercurrent of powerlessness and resentment. They want to scream at someone, but lack the courage and social awareness to do so. Therefore, their alienation and bitterness grows, and eventually they take action into their own hands in a way that they feel comfortable with. They always try to do things in a roundabout way because they cannot handle direct confrontation. They feel weak in such situations, which is why they always look for subtle ways to deliver an attack.

They subtly undermine the real or imagined object or person they resent. They mutter to themselves instead of confronting another person. They smile at you even though they're angry. They speak with sarcasm, double meanings, and veiled threats.

When passive-aggressive individuals communicate, they convey the following messages:

- I feel insecure with confrontation so I sabotage and disrupt.
- Why can't they understand what I'm feeling?
- I will appear cooperative on the outside,

but I secretly hope for your failure.
- I'm really angry, but I can't show it.
- You're stupid for not seeing my passive-aggressive hints and signs.
- I want to get my way, but I won't tell you what it is or how to get it. Figure it out.

Unlike the other two communicators, passive-aggressive communicators aren't driven solely by insecurity. They are driven by a combination of insecurity and deep bitterness about being overlooked by others. They feel they deserve better, but don't know how to express it. Most of the time, it simply appears clumsy and transparent.

Therefore, the way to deal with passive-aggressive communicators is to validate their feelings. Make it known that you've noticed their signs, even if you haven't and need to fabricate something to acknowledge, and ask them to clarify what you've missed and exactly what they want.

This way, they can feel that their underhanded tactics and maneuvers actually worked. This gives them exactly what they want—control and dominance over a situation without having to resort to confrontation. Everyone just wants to feel in control and right sometimes.

Assertive Communication

This last communication style happens to be the most ideal approach.

Assertive communicators clearly state their opinions and feelings and firmly advocate for their rights and needs.

What makes this different from aggressive communication is that there is no need to violate the rights of others. You objectively recognize what your rights are, and where the boundaries lie, and assert them as a matter of fact. You don't need to step on others to get yours.

Assertive communication is a result of high and healthy self-esteem. They know what they are worth and what they deserve and will not let others trample on them.

Assertive people value themselves, their time, and their emotional, spiritual, and physical needs. These types of people have chosen to be strong advocates for themselves while being respectful of the rights of others. They don't believe that for them to win, other people have to lose. On the other hand, they have no reservations about standing up for themselves and aren't uncomfortable with conflict when dealing with any of the other communication styles. The cost is worth the benefit for them.

Assertive people feel connected with others and they state their needs and feelings clearly, appropriately, and respectfully. They are in control of their emotions and speak in calm and clear tones. They are good listeners, maintain good eye contact, and create a respectful environment for others. They do not allow others to abuse or manipulate them.

When assertive people communicate with others, they convey the following messages:

- I am confident in who I am.
- I will make the best of this situation.
- I speak honestly and directly without ulterior motives.
- I know what I deserve and don't accept anything less.
- I have faults and admit them freely.
- I have boundaries and will not tolerate certain behavior.

How do you deal with assertive communicators? Well, hope that everyone you come across is one, because they are the easiest to speak to. There is no best practice because they are adaptable and can deal expertly with any communication style.

That's why this is the style to aspire to. They speak honestly and you don't get the sense that they're trying to accomplish something involving you behind your back.

Notably, they are not driven by the need to prove themselves or protect their self-perception. It's amazing what self-esteem can do, and it shows that if you are comfortable with yourself, others will be as well. It's the internal struggle of not feeling good enough and attempting to compensate that drives the negative aspects of other communication styles.

Assertive communicators walk the very thin line between agreeableness and having healthy boundaries.

Most people define being agreeable with some combination of the following: being accommodating, being adaptable, being flexible, and, perhaps above all else, letting other people have their way. Generally speaking, this can be a good thing, but there are problems with being agreeable all the time.

Agreeableness to the extreme leads to becoming a doormat. You don't want to be taken advantage of, and at times it can be difficult to draw the line and you can end up as a passive communicator. Unfortunately, many people who try to be agreeable fall into this exact trap. They blur the line for themselves, and all of a sudden, instead of mutually beneficial situations, they end up serving other people's self-interests and ignoring their own.

You need to be able to set boundaries to make sure this doesn't happen. You have to resolve to be looked at by other people as a person with your own agency and your own core principles. You can't simply allow yourself to be dismissed as a part of a mindless group of people that can easily be deceived, manipulated, or stepped on. So how do you navigate the balance between agreeableness and boundaries to form *agreeable boundaries*?

Boundaries are limits where you are not being taken advantage of in an unfair manner. Subjectively, they are limits to what you're willing to do or accommodate. To most, this is where we start to feel as if we're being used or manipulated. How do you have good boundaries but also remain agreeable and flexible at the same time? How do you maintain being agreeable while at the same time being assertive as to your needs?

People tend to fall on one side or the other, so

the best approach is to determine where you fall on the agreeableness-boundaries spectrum and work toward the middle. This will help you not only communicate in a more assertive fashion, but also frame your own priorities when they intersect with those of others.

Here's how to know if you need more boundaries:

- You fear awkwardness more than not having your way on something that's important to you.
- You avoid all conflict, even questions that are posed out of curiosity and are not requests.
- You constantly put other people's needs in front of your own.
- You always give people the benefit of the doubt.
- You don't like defending yourself or your choices against any type of criticism.
- You feel threatened and insecure when challenged.
- You are easily convinced or manipulated.
- You accept people's criticism immediately

and without question.
- You accommodate out of insecurity and fear of rejection.

If these seem like they hit home, you need to realize that people won't reject you or hate you just because you refuse what they want. If they lack the ability to separate the two, the fault is on them and they are acting out of turn, not you. You also have to separate yourself from a conflict about a situation, and people's feelings and emotions towards you. They likely won't change over small issues—really, any issue that isn't offensive or insulting won't change their feelings toward you.

If you feel like someone will lose their respect for you because of a simple disagreement, or someone might be upset at not getting their way for once—you need more boundaries. It comes down to breaking the assumptions of negativity that come along with a disagreement. We avoid these feelings for years, and it seems so simple to just let other people have their way. Sometimes it might be, but there is a cumulative effect that is enabling behavior on the part of both parties.

Remember that there is an objective and subjective component to the agreeableness-boundary line. Just make sure you aren't compromising everything in a subjective manner.

On the flip side, here's how to know if you need to be more agreeable:

- You see things in black or white.
- You think things like, "My way or the highway."
- You are unwilling to accommodate based on principle.
- You ignore other people's needs.
- You view your needs as more important.
- You feel that things will fall apart if you don't get your way.
- You don't recognize a difference between your way and the right way.
- You have rigid and arbitrary yes/no rules.
- You nitpick about details that don't matter.
- You are quickly dismissive of others.
- You feel the need to assert your opinion.

- You feel huge insecurity about being incorrect.

This is when you need to loosen up a little bit and start to bend with the wind more. In some rare occasions in the office, matters might truly be black and white. But especially in social situations, you need to bend if you want any semblance of charm or likability.

Very quickly, people will figure out that you only want your way, and that's the highway to nowhere—nowhere being a location where people don't want to spend time with you, and don't want to even speak to you.

People will respect you more if you are adaptable and not stuck in one mode of thinking. People don't generally like stubborn people. On the other hand, you don't want to be a doormat. Putting up too many boundaries will make you look selfish and rigid. On the other hand, if you are too agreeable, you open the way to being consistently taken advantage of.

Where does the balance truly lie? The answer is different for everyone. Most people fall more on one side of the spectrum but have a large degree of flexibility. Examine each situation from the objective measure of fairness. After that, think about whether you're acting out of your own accord or simply reacting to the relationship dynamic.

I would love to say that just by having identified these four styles, I can firmly put myself into the assertive communication category. But that's not always true, and it won't be true for you either.

And that's okay. We're all human, and no matter where on the spectrum you fall, (1) knowing that there is indeed a difference and (2) having a framework to understand their motivations and how to deal with them will help you immensely with people no matter the situation.

Chapter 9. Walk a Mile

Empathy is the ability to accurately put yourself in someone else's shoes and experience what they are feeling. When you can relate to someone, you can understand their motivations and behavior.

It sounds like a simple task—you just visualize how it might feel in your head and you are practically there, right? Not so. It's rare because most people either don't care enough, can only humor others in a superficial manner, or just don't possess a wide emotional range in the sense that we literally have never felt what someone else might be feeling.

But here's why getting beyond the shallow level of understanding is important. If you can't bother with empathy, it's like not knowing the difference in how to treat someone who's just come from a funeral, and someone who just attended a wedding. Most of the time, of course, it's much subtler than that. But empathy makes a significant difference in how comfortable and open people will feel around you. Empathy allows you to read people better and be on their exact emotional wavelength without them having to tell you.

How do you know how to interpret someone's sudden change in vocal tone, or the way that they closed the door? How do you know if someone is enjoying your company or not? How do you know if someone is really laughing at your jokes or just being polite? How can you truly get inside someone's head to understand how they are feeling?

Being a people person is about innately understanding as many perspectives as possible. The end result of having a highly tuned sense of empathy is that people will ask you in a rhetorical sense, "Do you know what I mean?" and you'll be able to put words and sentiments into their mouths. I can't emphasize how powerful this is in building a connection that goes deep.

However, as mentioned, it's not just a matter of thinking, "I wonder what this feels like?"

Let's take Patricia Moore, for example. She is a prime example of taking the extra step to understand others and thus be able to speak for them. Moore was an American designer who conducted an experiment in the 1970s that fundamentally changed people's notions about empathy.

What began as a social experiment quickly turned into something more. She, at the age of 26, dressed up as an 85-year-old woman to investigate what life was like for an elderly person—specifically, what were the challenges they faced as a result of old age, and how could those challenges be conquered?

On and off for three full years, Moore donned full makeup, walked with a limp to simulate arthritis, and wrapped herself in bandages to fake ailments and illnesses. To complete her transformation into an elderly person, she wore thick glasses that she couldn't see well out of. The illusion was complete.

In this guise, she visited many cities and acted as an elderly woman might. She rode public transportation, navigated stores, and generally tried her hand at everyday life, essentially handicapped by her advanced age and various ailments.

Based on her experiences, she walked away with a profoundly new perspective on product design. It turned out that designs in America are focused predominantly on people who are younger and more able.

Can openers, doors, and other modern amenities were bundled up with all sorts of assumptions regarding physical ability. These products were designed for those who are in the prime of their lives. They are not very friendly to children and they were definitely outright hostile to the physical limitations of elderly Americans. They were not very accommodating or convenient for those with simple ailments such as weak hands or poor eyesight.

Based on these experiences and her difficulties, she came up with new product designs that can be used by elderly people. For example, instead of regular potato peelers with thin handles, she padded these with thick rubber to enable older people with reduced grips to use them comfortably.

She also invented new kitchen products that can easily be used by people suffering from arthritis. Based on her three-year experience, she became one of the most outspoken and prominent elderly rights advocates in the United States. Thanks, in large part, to her own personal efforts at understanding modern life from the perspective of an older American, the Americans with Disabilities Act (ADA) was passed.

Her latest project is designing rehabilitation centers for U.S. war veterans with missing limbs or brain injuries so they can relearn to live independently, doing everything from buying groceries to using a cash machine.

What can be learned from Moore's experience in the pursuit of empathy?

By simply choosing to walk a mile in another person's shoes, we begin to see the world in a very different way. We also begin to detect our unconscious biases. Take a regular can opener; most people would not think twice about using a can opener with a thin handle, but if you were an older person with arthritis and mobility issues, it can be quite a challenge. Moore broke through these personal barriers that are often unspoken and invisible by assuming the physical limitations of another person.

Her experience is a powerful testimony to how well we can improve ourselves and the world around us by simply choosing to be open-minded and actively seeking to look at the world through the eyes of people we, at least on the surface, don't have much in common with. You have to seek out ways you can play out Moore's experiment in your life.

For example, what are the struggles that your friends or coworkers are going through? Suppose one of them is going through a divorce. It's worth visualizing the struggles in that, and even doing some research so you understand them better. But go beyond that starting point. What do their daily triumphs and struggles look like? There are certain triggers and anxieties associated with divorce, not to mention created by it, and you would relate to them exponentially better if you just engaged in this thought exercise from time to time.

Seek out ways you can do this in your life with the people around you. What about them don't you understand or are completely ignorant about? Remedy your ignorance. Understanding means that you're not just guessing or winging it—it means that you can succeed with people in whatever way you wish.

Talk to people and try to detect the assumptions they hold. Ask them questions that can relate to past experiences that might explain why they believe what they believe. While these opinions may normally be annoying, offensive, or ridiculous to you, the more you look at things from their perspective, the more things will make sense to you. Not only will you become a better conversationalist, you'll become a better person to be around.

By simply choosing to be more selfless and curious about others' perspectives, you will actually start to understand people. There's a big difference between understanding others and simply guessing. When you guess, you're still stuck with your own personal biases and stereotypes. Understanding can only come from actually experiencing or viewing things from another person's truly distinct perspective.

Compassion

Closely related to and sometimes confused with empathy is the concept of compassion. Compassion is the ability to feel concern and investment for other people's suffering.

Again, we possess this in obvious cases, such as when a good friend loses a family member.

It's easy to feel bad for and look out for people who matter to you—people in your tight familial and social circle. But human beings occupy many different concentric circles. The further out the circle people are, the less concerned about them we become. In some cases, our concern drops off a cliff.

For some people, if somebody falls outside of their family and friend circle, they could not care less. For others, the focus is more on their country or ethnic and religious group, and everybody outside that group doesn't get much consideration. Everybody has different levels of concern they show compassion towards.

Compassion, in an ideal sense, is your ability to put yourself in other people's shoes regardless of what they look like, regardless of what they believe, regardless of whether they believe in God or not, or which god they believe in, and regardless of whether they're male, female, or patriotic. As long as they're human beings, the ideal vision of compassion is being able to feel other people's pain. Easier said than done.

This isn't a trait to cultivate just to cultivate. It's what will allow you to genuinely relate to people in a different way. It changes you into a people person.

How would it feel?

Imagine that a loved one is suffering, something terrible has happened to him or her. Try to imagine the pain they are going through and look at the world through their eyes.

How would it feel?

Imagine yourself in their shoes trying to do things that you normally do, like going to the bathroom, getting up and walking around, or picking up the paper— the daily mundanities of normal life that we take for granted.

Can you feel the pain they are going through? Can you feel the uncertainty, the sheer terror, the regret, or the guilt? Try to subject yourself to the barrage of negative emotions that they must be going through.

This may seem exhausting, and it is, but if you practice this for a couple of weeks, you will be better able to imagine the suffering of other people you know.

You'll be surprised how open-minded you will become. You will also realize that there's really not much that divides us, and that's an important concept—focusing on similarities of circumstance and emotion.

For example, it's easy for somebody who is earning a lot of money to expect that everybody else should have a certain standard of living and should view the world a certain way. It's easy for us to live in our own bubbles. The same also applies in reverse. If you have always struggled, it's very easy to assume that everybody else is struggling too, and is looking at the world the way you do.

By practicing compassion, you destroy all those artificial barriers and you truly understand that we all bleed red. We all hunger. We all thirst. We all need love and meaning in our lives. Recognizing this similarity is at the center of true compassion. Instead of focusing on the differences between yourself and others, try to recognize that all these differences are just illusions. One of the best ways to get at this is to just look at what unites us.

Despite our differences and language, the way we choose to dress, the way we talk, and how we deal with certain issues, we all are driven by the same things. We have the same basic drive for food, water, sex, respect, protection, assurance—you name it.

The root of compassion lies in the things that

unite us instead of the things that separate us.

In the 1940s, psychologist Abraham Maslow came up with a concept called the "Hierarchy of Needs." According to this school of psychology, humanity has several needs and all psychological emotional personality issues are really reflections of whatever dysfunctions we have in meeting these needs. We are all the same, just with different levels of needs at any given time.

The most basic level, of course, is simple subsistence and self-preservation. You don't want to starve or die. We all share this.

Beyond that basic need is a need to do something with our lives, to achieve something. People have a need to prove to themselves that they are capable of making things happen—that they're capable of taking things they think about and turning their ideas into things they can see, hear, smell, touch, and taste.

Going beyond that level is a need for social

acclaim. It simply feels good to realize that other people are paying attention to what you're doing and rewarding you with validation. The highest form of this, of course, is love.

These have thus far all been relatively selfish pursuits. Maslow proposed that the highest need is when we're able to finally break out of this prison of the self—when we're able to transcend and stop focusing on what's important to us or how people view us (self-centered pursuits), and focus more on universal truths like justice, fairness, kindness, and truly seeking others not because they are reflections of our own needs, but because they are ends in and of themselves.

This is the fullest manifestation of compassion, and it happens to be a drive we all share. Look at someone you feel you have nothing in common with, or even that you actively dislike. Regardless of whatever hurtful thing that person has said or done, you share the same concerns at the end of the day. But they might be caught at the lower stages of self-centered pursuits.

Imagine what their daily struggles entail. Now imagine that you're the one going through that suffering. Think about how much you would like that suffering to end, and how grateful and happy you would be to someone who helped you, or maybe simply paid attention to you. That's a feeling that can be developed.

Hostile or negative actions are so rarely about you, and almost always about what people are going through themselves. It's easy to lose sight of someone's positive qualities when they lash out at you, but when that feeling strikes, attempt to remind yourself of at least one or two positive qualities that you admire about them. Humanize them and don't reduce them to a single act that had nothing to do with you.

In the end, real compassion has nothing to do with you or your own needs. It has nothing to do with your gratifying yourself, making yourself look good, or feeling fulfilled.

Real compassion is when you finally break

through the bonds of selfishness and self-absorption, and truly focus on somebody else's needs. You may have noticed this to be the general theme of the chapter. Whatever the name and approach you want to apply to it—empathy, compassion—it's clear that we are often too selfish and in our own heads to effectively connect with others.

The Platinum Rule

We even unwittingly apply this selfish approach when we try to combat it. For instance, the standard rule when it comes to being kind is the Golden Rule. The Golden Rule is, of course, *to treat others the way you want to be treated*.

Shouldn't we make it about how other people want to be treated? The Golden Rule sounds like a nice concept but really falls apart upon a closer look.

We all have different standards of good, bad, and acceptable. It's decidedly inefficient and plain weird when we try to apply a single standard, even if it is our own, to others. Is there a better way to approach others?

The Platinum Rule: treat others how they want to be treated.

It sounds simple, but this mentality has the ability to transform your interactions. The Golden Rule, for its positive intentions, is a self-centered way of viewing other people. When deciding how to act toward others, you aren't giving them a second thought. Instead, you are assuming that people are similar to you and think the same way; you are attributing or imposing your thoughts onto them. This assumes that you are a reasonable person with normal sensibilities, which also might not be the case.

It's why you so often hear things like, "Why are you so annoyed? You know I was joking. That's just my sense of humor!" Yes, and you expected other people to either conform or innately understand you.

One of the keys to being better with people

and being better liked is to wipe the slate clean and assume that you don't know how others want to be treated. When you start viewing people from their own perspective, instead of your own, you will get better results.

Suppose you are rich and are giving your friend Jonathan a present at his birthday party. Since you like rich, lavish gifts, you might assume that Jonathan does as well. But Jonathan is decidedly conservative with money, and lives in a poor neighborhood where things are stolen frequently.

In this case, treating someone the way you wish to be treated doesn't make the most sense, and also doesn't serve that person well. We're all wearing blinders that are made from our self-interests, past experiences, and backgrounds.

Unfortunately, our blinders can sometimes be strapped so tightly that we start looking at all the other people around us as extensions of ourselves. We start looking at situations as opportunities to advance our own agendas instead of simply taking a step back and asking what someone else might think about it.

The Golden Rule embodies another problem: what if you don't respect yourself very much? What if you have a poor opinion of yourself, and don't take care of yourself mentally or physically? What if you believe that the world is cruel and no one deserves any sympathy or help? This would be a poor mentality to carry over to others.

The Platinum Rule produces much better results because you are forced to step into other people's shoes. Let go of the "one size fits all" social template that you have previously been using.

For example, there is a new parent in your office. You are young, unmarried, and without a child. When you engage them, you have zero interest in talking about children. The Golden Rule would direct you away from the topic of children, but the Platinum Rule would ask what they would want to talk about. Guess what? It would be children.

One of the most valuable exercises for developing this kind of empathy is to read fiction and articulate exactly what the characters are feeling and why. This allows you to completely ignore yourself, because you're a character, and focus on the nuanced desires of people. If the book is well-written, you might be able to predict the plot from a combination of the personalities of the characters and the plot turns.

In some respect, this chapter might seem like it just tells you to ignore your own desires and turn yourself into a puppet for other people. In a sense, that's true.

People will always respond better to things they can relate to or that are about them. But it's not manipulative or pandering to take advantage of that knowledge. Instead, it shows people that you're different, and that there are easier roads into people's hearts.

Chapter 10. The Value of Shutting Up

We often think of people who are talkative and outgoing as some of the most skilled socializers there are, as they can prevent awkward silences and make others more comfortable by shouldering the brunt of the social burden in a given situation.

This chapter, however, is about the value of having a filter when you speak and understanding when it's time to simply shut up. At one time or another, everybody will eventually experience times when silence is appropriate, as well as times when an acquaintance, friend, or partner just needs somebody to listen to them talk for a little while.

There won't be any scientific studies in this chapter, because knowing when it's best to stay quite is mostly a matter of developing strong intuition, perception, and common sense. Having a big mouth can land you into some really big trouble, so it is greatly important to know what *not* to say and when *not* to make your presence known.

Pick Your Battles

One of the easiest mistakes for people to make socially is to get so attached to their ideas and thoughts that they are willing to harm their relationships for the sake of being "right." This is especially common in the case of interpersonal conflicts, when we are more emotionally sensitive and vulnerable and thus less likely to think clearly and rationally.

Have you ever said a lot of things that you thought were important in the heat of the moment, only to realize a few minutes or maybe days afterwards that it really didn't matter that much? Or worse, have you ever realized that you damaged a relationship with somebody you care about because you let your emotions carry you away?

Sometimes the best thing that we can do for ourselves is to relax a bit and to get in the habit of letting things slide instead of taking everything too seriously. We simply don't need to make every argument at every opportunity, and doing so is detrimental to our social success.

With a little introspection, you might also realize that you argue passionately over perceived transgressions—not because of the transgressions themselves—but because they hurt your sense of pride. Naturally, you're a lot more likely to say something regrettable when you're feeling insecure or threatened, as those fear-associated feelings lead to instinct overriding reason. By practicing mindfulness and self-awareness, however, you can cut off these harmful defense patterns and avoid saying things you'll regret later on.

You might be thinking that it's not always that

straightforward to pick your battles, however.

You'd be right, sometimes the correct decision between being agreeable or being assertive isn't that obvious. You need to know when to shut up and when to stand your ground, and when that line is blurry, you'll need to rely on awareness and experience to determine a course of action. Asking yourself whether this will matter to you 30 days from now can be a really simple way to assess the importance of speaking up.

And for those times when it just isn't worth it, one of the best ways to avoid unnecessary conflict is by pretending not to hear what others have said. When you choose to be the bigger person and keep the peace instead of getting emotional, you show maturity and self-confidence that will improve your perception among other socially skilled people.

Imagine that you overhear a colleague at work saying that they are better at the job than you. Either they have a good point and you should focus on improving your work, or they are insecure about their own job and trying to feel better by putting you down, in which case confronting them is probably going to go poorly. Your colleagues likely don't appreciate being brought into other people's drama, so being defensive and talking to them isn't expected to win you any likeability points there, either. But not saying anything, and just doing well at your job? That makes the bad-mouth look illegitimate and wins you respect among your peers because you showed maturity and professionalism.

You'll save yourself a lot trouble in life if you just shut up and accept that you won't always get things your way.

Listen More and Brag Less

All of us are self-interested to an extent, some much more so than others. Keeping this in mind when we socialize can make a world of difference in how likeable we are and how much people want to foster relationships with us.

The first way to utilize an awareness of this human trait is to appease other people's desire to talk about themselves by listening to them and showing interest in what they are talking about. This makes the conversation enjoyable for the person you are talking to, and also gives them social validation, which makes them feel good about sharing their thoughts with you. That's exactly what you want! Give them the spotlight and provide encouragement as they open up so that they can gain confidence in themselves and trust in you.

The people whom you like best and choose to spend time with most often are very likely the people who make you feel the best in their company. Feeling comfortable and accepted allows us to express ourselves openly, which naturally leaves a better impression than feeling awkward, judged, or bored. You can use this to your advantage by being genuinely curious about people you meet or already know, and seeing what you can learn from listening to what they have to say.

Suppose that you're making small talk with a

new acquaintance, and they start venting about their work. Sounds like it will be an unpleasant interaction, right? Now you can half-listen to them for the sake of politeness and then interrupt as quickly as possible, or you can take a sincere interest in them and try to make a connection. You might try to learn why they are unhappy with their work, and what they would rather be doing instead. By being engaged, you at least give yourself the chance to steer the conversation from a negative subject to a passion or an interest they have, which will make them feel better and will hopefully be more enjoyable for you too.

On the other side of the coin, we have the braggers—the people who just won't shut up about their accomplishments and how amazing they are. You want to do everything you can to not be one of these people, because just about everybody finds excessive bravado annoying.

Something that people who brag a lot often don't realize is that it leaves others with an impression that you are overcompensating and that you lack vulnerability—making it more difficult to connect with you. Additionally, boasting will give the appearance that you are trying to be someone you are not—an unconfident look that a lot of people will see straight through. Braggers also tend to be sensitive to criticism and overly defensive, which only adds to the unpleasantness of their company.

Perhaps the most annoying thing that a bragger will do is constantly try to one-up other people. Let's say somebody is really excited about losing 15 pounds and getting into better shape, and instead of congratulating or encouraging them, you start talking about your own fitness accomplishments and steal all of the thunder. Frankly, nobody cares about how fit you are, and this doesn't make you look cool at all. It just makes everybody think you're self-centered and rude, and it might be dejecting to the person who was excited about their weight loss.

As a general rule, you'll be perceived more

positively by others when you make the effort to listen more often than you talk and to show real interest in what other people have to say. A little pat on your own back every now and again doesn't hurt, but if you are constantly talking yourself up, it's going to be counterproductive for achieving more social success.

So remember to just shut up about yourself because, even though you might see yourself as the center of the universe, other people don't.

Stop With "Brutal" Honesty and Stop Giving Unsolicited Advice

How many times have you heard somebody excuse rude and hurtful comments by claiming that they are simply calling it how they see it, or being brutally honest? Chances are you've come across a few people who communicate this way, and it's also probable that they weren't the most likable people you've ever encountered.

Brutal honesty most often means criticizing others without any tact or sense of compassion. Supposedly, those blunt comments and criticisms are meant to be beneficial to whomever they are directed at, and they are only hurtful if taken personally or defensively.

The thing about brutal honesty, though, is that nobody actually prefers it, and in most cases, it just comes across as deliberately mean. The vast majority of the time, negativity just isn't necessary because it's possible to accomplish your goal by providing feedback or criticism in a mature and considerate way. Complaining and nitpicking about things that aren't important just makes you come across as judgmental and abrasive—making others feel small so that you can feel big.

Honesty itself is very useful, and having the tact to be honest in a way that doesn't put people down is an invaluable life skill to have. But far too many people think that honesty is socially acceptable in any form. The simple truth of the matter is that if you want to always say how you feel without any kind of a filter, people just won't like you. Unless, of course, you are the first brutally honest person ever to think and feel positive things all the time.

There's a particular type of brutal honesty, tough love, that's commonly used by parents to teach their young children important lessons. But tough love is not for everyone or every situation, and is probably even counterproductive for raising children in a lot of scenarios, as the lesson they learn may come with an unhealthy hit to their self-esteem.

Anytime that you feel the need to criticize somebody, ask if that criticism can actually help them. If not, keep it to yourself. If so, frame it in a tactful way that doesn't come off as a personal attack.

For example, say you've got a friend who dresses really poorly and it adversely affects their attractiveness to others. If that's something your friend cares about and would want to know, then a productive way to help your friend is to suggest something that you think would look good on them, and then compliment them when they do dress well in order to give positive reinforcement. Except in serious cases, positive reinforcement can work a whole lot better than criticism—especially criticism that's framed as honesty, but lacking any practical advice.

But now let's imagine that your friend has never given any indication that they want to improve their attractiveness or that they care about their wardrobe. Now anything you say in the form of advice is unsolicited, which just makes you annoying.

As a general rule, giving unsolicited advice isn't going to be received well, no matter how good your intentions are. When people vent or rant to you about some problems in their lives, the socially intelligent response is to let them fulfill their purpose for speaking without interrupting them to interject your own solution. Talking about problems serves as emotional catharsis—meaning that it's often a solution all of its own, and you can be a part of that solution just by listening.

Finally, one of the most socially counterproductive things you can do is to make pedantic corrections of people. Anything that indirectly implies that you are above others will make you less likeable, plain and simple. You may think that people want or should want to be corrected when they error, but when those errors are unimportant and don't hurt anybody, it's not your responsibility or social prerogative to point them out.

So do yourself and everybody else a favor—shut up and stop interjecting your opinions and advice when nobody asks or cares to hear them.

The common theme from each of these social mistakes that people make is that they can be avoided just by shutting up more often. You may only exhibit one or two of these behaviors personally, or even none of them if you are already highly skilled socially. It's also possible that, through introspection, you could realize you are guilty of almost all of them from time to time.

It's good to analyze when you've made these mistakes in the past, as it can show the areas that you should personally focus on building more awareness in the future. That being said, there's no use in beating yourself up over those mistakes, because we all do these things to some degree. Not knowing when to shut up doesn't automatically make you unlikable; it simply inhibits you from reaching your full social potential.

If you build your awareness about when it's appropriate to talk and when it's better to listen or be silent, you'll improve the depth of your relationships and be more enjoyable company for the people in your life. In the famous words of the 19th century actor Will Rogers, "Never miss a good chance to shut up."

Chapter 11. Connect Instantly

If you want to connect with people faster and infiltrate your environment more efficiently and more effectively, you need to adopt the right mindset towards the people around you.

Your ability to connect with people and gain acceptance is a reflection of your attitude. If you think new people or social situations are scary, chances are you are not going to connect that well with unfamiliar people. You are either going to avoid them or act in a way that makes you come off as standoffish, nervous, or uncomfortable. People will react accordingly.

The key lesson of this chapter is that your

mental perception dictates your external reality. What you perceive the world and others to be will in fact happen. This is because whatever attitude you show to the world determines the type of feedback you get and build from.

There are a few approaches that will assist you in your quest for rapport and consistently garner positive feedback from others.

Care

Think along these lines: I wonder what *they* are like. What can they teach me? What do we have in common? What are they great at and what can I learn from them?

Ask yourself these questions. When you meet new people, feel the positive emotions that they carry. Convince yourself that they are valuable and fascinating. Make it your mission to find out everything you possibly can about them. It's the only way you can force yourself to care if you're not naturally interested and curious in people.

When you think about these attitudes, there's no reason to think they aren't true. We're not always the best at everything we try our hand at, and we're not all that and a bag of chips. Other people have at least five things that they can teach us about in a pinch—make it your mission and attitude to find those things and gain value from others, as well as impart your own.

Even if you are feeling apprehensive and insecure or have low self-esteem and low self-confidence, block out those negative signals and just let the questions carry you. By fostering a genuine sense of curiosity and adventure to push you forward, you can connect easily and quickly with people.

If you don't actually think that other people are interesting or can provide you anything of value (be it just information or entertainment), then you are likely to act that way and not establish any sort of connection. As mentioned, you get back what you put into the world, and when people sense your disinterest, they will reflect it back to you. You might feel like you have encountered boring people all day, but if you decide that they are boring, you are actually the boring one because you don't try to engage them in any meaningful way.

Everyone is worth your time—though not necessarily at first glance, so you will benefit from digging and discovering.

Caring is something you must proactively do. What about an act to proactively avoid? This isn't necessarily a toxic habit, rather just an approach that will lower your chances of making a connection.

Banish Goals

If you go into an interaction with a specific goal, chances are things are not going to pan out because you will project a poor attitude.

Your goals create pretense and pressure on the entire interaction. Some of us aren't good at keeping secrets, and it will show, as you will care less about getting to know someone than getting to your goal. Sometimes a focused goal is beneficial, but it can also make you oblivious to potential pathways for connection while in pursuit of that goal. In other words, because you're too focused on X, you miss the opportunities for Y and Z, opportunities that might have been extremely fruitful on their own.

Similarly, if you lead into interactions with any type of expectations or pressure on yourself, instead of seeming excited and welcoming, you will come off as brusque, insensitive, or calculated and scheming. This will also seep into the air that you project in your social situation—people with expectations are all about what they receive, not what they give. People are often more astute than you might think, and people will catch on to this attitude that you emanate.

Practice

The next time you go out to a café or to a store, focus on working on your ability to establish a genuine connection. It may feel extremely unfamiliar. You can do this by working with a member of a captive audience. I am, of course, talking about people who work at the café or store. The Starbucks barista or the store cashier doesn't have any place to go. That's their job. They are supposed to interact with you and laugh at your jokes.

And the best part is they are required to be nice to you. So even if you fall flat on your face trying to make a quick personal connection, it won't matter because you will not feel the sting of rejection or mockery because these people are paid to be nice to you. Once you are in front of one of them, and they have the space and time to entertain you, ask them how they are. Ask them how their day is going and what they think of the day's news.

Give them your full attention and work on caring, not coming to the table with a goal in mind, and just listening only to what someone says. Practice. Try to catch yourself when you turn the topic back to you, and start to form the habit of curiosity and interest. Ask five questions in a row. Dig deep and find the nitty-gritty details on one topic you previously did not care about. Discover where your barista or cashier was born and raised.

Above all else, see what happens when you throw your preconceptions and ulterior motives out the window and just see a human being across from you.

And what happens if you feel that you falter in the conversation and embarrass yourself? Nothing. That's the best part. These people are paid to be nice to you. You can try again tomorrow, and the day after, and the day after that—until you succeed. It's a safe environment for you to practice and emerge with greater confidence.

Negativity

We've all had people in our lives who are emotional black holes.

They'll call you up when they're feeling depressed or upset and unload for hours. They might not even ask how you are, and when they've finished, they'll suddenly be too busy to continue the conversation and give you a chance to talk.

At conversation's end, I feel negative and dragged into an emotional mess, but they feel much lighter and better. I want to be there for them, but if I allow myself to be just a sounding board, I eventually start absorbing some of their negativity and see the world in dark tones.

Thankfully, it dawned on me that in order to help them, I did not have to assume the same negativity. Good people skills can be used to cut tension, relieve depression and despair, and smooth over matters that create or prolong negative emotions and anger.

Instead of passively listening and absorbing their negativity like a sponge, act as mediator.

This is similar to active listening, where you are using their words and in actuality doing very little except providing an empty canvas for them to fill with their own thoughts.

Be the one that guides them through their misery and helps them discover what truly upsets them. It's true that some people talk through their negativity out loud to others as a catharsis and aren't actually seeking a solution, but that takes a toll on you, especially if it's the same people with the same issues time after time.

The first step is to help them realize why they are upset in the first place. There are the obvious reasons, such as someone being broken up with. But the less obvious and perhaps more important reasons are the ones you'll have to ferret out, such as someone's fear of loneliness or insecurity. There may be a seemingly obvious cause of despair, but in reality, the issue might be caused by something completely unrelated. It might even come right out of left field. This is part intuition and part listening.

Second, most causes of negativity and depression are because of an insecurity of some sort. However, most of us have stalwart defense mechanisms and may never reach this level of radical self-honesty—but it is necessary for people to truly understand what is happening to them.

Attempt to create a safe space for someone to admit true insecurities. This allows you to address them and really work on them, as opposed to beat around them and work on things they know won't truly make a difference in your negativity.

You can prompt this with leading statements like, "It sounds like you were feeling insecure about X, or like your friends might have been leaving you behind..."

The third step is prompting for solution. Remember, at this point, we aren't dealing with someone who just wants a listening ear. We're dealing with someone who has a pattern of negativity in their lives that shouldn't continue being placated.

How do you prompt for solution? Thankfully, it doesn't involve you having to generate idea after idea. The funny part about negativity is most people know deep down inside what needs to be done. They just need to articulate it to themselves and take ownership of it. You can help them along with leading questions such as "What do you think needs to happen now? Is it something you can do? What about this?"

Try to come away from this conversation with at least one concrete step to put into action. This way, you can occasionally turn negativity into accomplishment and avoid absorbing the negativity.

Mediation doesn't always work because many people just aren't open to it. They aren't ready to hear it, or they don't want to admit any fault or blame. If mediation falls upon deaf ears, try distraction.

What you're really doing is diverting attention from an issue that has gotten out of hand. The key here is to distract them long enough so that the emotional tension subsides sufficiently for you to either have a mature discussion or forget about it altogether. It's nearly impossible to use facts and logic when people are reacting emotionally. If people are on the verge of strangling each other, all the facts, logic, and expert arguing in the world are not going to matter all that much.

Once it's gone or sufficiently reduced, you can attempt to turn back into mediation mode. Your main job is not to convince them. Your main job is not to overpower them. Your main job is to make them feel that you're listening to them to such an extent that they can get rid of the negative atmosphere.

Sometimes people just need to stick their heads into a pillow and scream, but other times they need help finding clarity.

Ethos, Pathos, and Logos

Don't let the Latin throw you off.

Ethos, pathos, and logos are a slightly different framework to understand people better. It is a framework developed by the Greek philosopher Aristotle, and in one form or another, it has been around for thousands of years. In other words, it's proven.

Even though the concept of self-interest gives us a healthy blueprint to predicting and understanding behavior, there are other important factors to consider. This method of thought leverages the three most powerful motivations people have outside of themselves: the ethos, pathos, and logos. Ethos refers to ethical concerns, pathos to emotional concerns, and logos to reason and logical concerns. What matters when people make decisions and what do they base their judgments off of? Well, we make logical, emotional, and ethical considerations.

Ethos, pathos, and logos are typically mentioned in the context of argumentation and persuasion. It's not hard to see how they apply to social interaction because of the understanding they provide.

An appeal to ethos is when you address the fact that people care about your character. In other words, people look at the source of a statement or argument, and act corresponding to how trustworthy or powerful they feel the source is. The argument is that you are trustworthy and sound, and would never steer someone wrong. If your character is credible and trustworthy enough, then they have every reason to like you or even follow your lead.

How do you make an argument about your character? It usually comes from your past experience or knowledge. "I've never steered you wrong in the past, have I?" or "I've done this 100 times in the past; don't worry."

Maybe you come from a good pedigree or you come from a very prestigious institution. You can also use your track record. Maybe you have shown that you are a fair and unbiased person who makes the right call every single time. Maybe you've always carried yourself with dignity and class. The key takeaway here is that your power to convince the person you are trying to persuade revolves around your character. Known quantities are the best.

As for pathos, have you heard of the words pathetic, sympathetic, and psychopath? All these words share the same Latin root, which is pathos. Pathos is emotion.

When you make an appeal to pathos, you are appealing to people's emotions and are, by definition, not making a logical argument. You are depending on being able to take advantage of someone's emotional instability to win them over.

You can either generate an emotional response in people to sway them, or you can capitalize on an existing emotional trigger point and harness it for your own purposes.

Make people forget reality and logic. Use hyperbole and colorful, illustrative language that induces people to think outside the box of possibility. Craft emotional and intense stories to shortcut people's logic and engage their emotions. Make it personal to them, in a way that almost forces them to react in self-defense. Above all, make them feel involved and affected.

Think about the television commercials that show sad-looking dogs and cats in deplorable living conditions. They are the epitome of an appeal to emotions because they make you feel so personally involved that you act with a donation or adoption. These commercials are undoubtedly more effective than they would be if they simply stated the pros and cons adopting or donating to their organization. More of our daily decisions are based on emotional triggers than we would like to admit.

Finally, logos is when you try to convince an audience by using logic and reasoning.

Straight appeals to logic are very easy to see. You can see somebody appealing to your reasoning ability when they lay out an assertion and then support their assertion with facts. Truly brilliant argumentation breaks it down even further. They take the facts and then come up with different readings, either for or against their assertion, and then they knock down the objections raised by those facts.

There is a high degree of structure, and appealing to someone's sense of logos almost reads like a scientific study. Logic dictates carefully analyzing the pros and cons and then making a decision based on them.

An appeal to logos is what every other motivation attempts to pass itself off as. They look as if they are making a sound argument by appealing to logic and reason, but in reality, they are playing all sorts of tricks to prevent the audience from making a logical decision.

Connecting instantly, or at all for that matter, is not as simple as talking about the weather. However, it can be made much easier if you focus on a few mindsets that make you open, accepting, and emotionally aware as a byproduct.

Chapter 12. Workplace Tactics

As important as you might assume interpersonal skills and people tactics are in your personal life, they can make or break you at the office and sabotage your livelihood.

In our social and personal lives, we generally choose people whom we like and enjoy being around. It's no accident whom we spend time with, and we simply avoid those we don't have anything in common with.

Of course, this is the opposite of a working environment. The only thing you might have in common with your cubicle mate might be the fact that you both applied to the same company at around the same time. These people might be fundamentally different than you, but your career trajectory is greatly impacted by how well you get along with them.

To make things even more difficult, the workplace is fraught with situations that are tense, confrontational, or just plain uncomfortable. It's what happens in an environment where people are objectively evaluated on performance under a clear hierarchy.

Telling a coworker that he smells? Sitting someone down and letting them know that their work just isn't up to snuff? What if you have to fire someone?

It doesn't matter how smart or how well intentioned you are; no one excels in the office in a vacuum. Beyond being likable and a pleasant person to be around, you need to know how to handle the uncomfortable situations that will inevitably arise. Some might call this dealing with *office politics*, but in reality, it's just excelling in whatever social situation you find yourself in.

If you put in 100 units of effort toward interpersonal skills for social situations, you should put in 500 units in the workplace because of the greater consequences. If you don't feel that there are *positive* consequences from being better with coworkers and supervisors, then you are truly not realizing your potential in the office.

There are a few main tactics you must learn to employ in the office for better likability and workplace cachet.

Conflict Management

Even if you're not a manager or a supervisor, you need this ability. Regardless of your label or title, it thrusts you into the leader position organically. People will begin to rally around you when they have problems of any sort, and you just may become the "go-to" person when personal conflicts arise.

It's only a matter of time until your supervisors and managers recognize this and you get promoted. What is the best way to manage conflict?

Look at the arguments of each side and try to name three things that they each want. Instead of competing over the one objective, they now have three ways for them to gain a happy resolution from the conflict. Most conflict stems from either an emotional reaction or a fundamental misunderstanding.

For example, often people just want validation, credit, or recognition. This is something we take for granted that motivates others. What if you discovered someone was truly looking for that as opposed to the same promotion as you?

Use your creativity, your intelligence, and the information you know about the parties involved to craft win-win resolutions instead of naming a black-or-white winner and loser. This is not going to happen unless you effectively respect differences of opinions. Acting as the mediator may even just boil down to getting two parties to sit down and speak without malice or screaming.

Accountability

In any organization, there will always be people who try to make themselves look better by shifting the blame to others.

For example, a new marketing director starts a job and figures out that she is in over her head. So what does she do? She blames the previous marketing director and paints such a terrible picture that the CEO accepts the new marketing director's dismal results as an improvement.

The people who matter will take notice of this kind of behavior. It's not that you're not holding yourself to high standards; it's that you refuse to take responsibility for your actions, and instead make it the fault of anyone but yourself. This is the compulsion to make excuses because (1) you are insecure and don't want to face the truth or (2) you are selfish and have no problem putting others down to keep yourself afloat. Neither are attractive traits.

They both paint the picture of someone who is incredibly unreliable and cares only about their own image to the detriment of everything else. You also create discomfort when working with others because they'll never be sure if you will throw them under the bus to benefit yourself. Overall, if you don't take responsibility and hold yourself accountable for your own actions, you end up as a big question mark in people's minds. If you can't acknowledge reality, what else will you misrepresent or lie about?

Instead, take full responsibility and look at your obstacles or failures as a personal challenge to your creativity and intellect. Admit shortcomings or wrongdoings, and only then can you actually work towards rectifying what went wrong. There is much truth in the sentiment that failure is the best teacher because it won't lie and it will tell you exactly what you need to hear to *not fail*.

Taking responsibility for negative instances will also make your triumphs and achievements that much more satisfying and significant to those who monitor such things.

Appreciation

This can be as simple as saying, "Thank you" or "Great job," but it's something that is missing more often than not in our workplace relationships.

Just because it is someone's job to deliver you a pizza doesn't mean they won't feel good if you voice appreciation for it and praise them. You have to let other people know you value them and their help. Just because a person is low on the totem pole doesn't mean they are worthless. Each and every one of them works so that you can focus on what you bring to the table, no matter how high- or low-value it is.

Let others know that you appreciate and value their usefulness. By simply being appreciative and being genuine about it, you can go a long way in becoming a source of emotional reassurance in your organization. Don't assume it's natural, unspoken, or implied. Say it loudly and directly.

For example, if one of your subordinates brings you a report you asked for on a tight deadline, you could take them aside and thank them for working long hours and tell them how much you appreciate the work they put in, and that your work would be impossible without them, and that their superiors will definitely know about their work.

No one ever gets tired of gratitude or appreciation. Make it a habit of yours and it will become infectious through your office like the flu. Especially powerful is when you show appreciation and praise in front of other people, coworkers and supervisors alike. It builds a congenial and encouraging workplace culture and creates multiple sources of positivity instead of just you. Finally, it's a driving source of positive conditioning.

Leadership

In any organization, there are always two types of leaders: formal and organic leaders. Formal leaders are the people you see on an organizational chart. People will look at you as a leader not necessarily because they want to, but because they have to. When it comes to crunch time and things that really matter as far as the day-to-day operations of any organization, the success of any firm or outfit depends on how many organic leaders there are.

When I was in college, I worked a few side jobs for extra money. All the jobs I had after I got my degree followed this pattern. I notice that when I entered the doors, there were always "official" leaders and "organic" leaders.

Organic leaders are people whom coworkers instinctively and naturally flock around. When it comes to forming an opinion or expressing the sentiments of coworkers or collaborating regarding an event or solving an issue, my coworkers always went to the same handful of people.

By improving your people skills, organic leadership will naturally follow. Improve your organic leadership by listening with intent. Don't speak with a set agenda. Instead, pay close attention to what people are saying and then try to get to the bottom of why people have a certain issue in mind.

Is it something they want to solve? Should someone else be involved? Do they just want to be heard? If people are all worked up about a certain person or a problem, ask questions that are not judgmental in nature but reveal why people feel the way they do. Give people an opportunity to get stuff off their chest, but also direct the person's sharing. In addition, make it safe for others to share and be vulnerable by suspending judgment.

You should also always seek to create a two-way dialogue. Ask more questions than you answer. For every response or story you tell, you can seek to ask two questions to keep it semi-balanced.

Take an interest in other people and stop being self-centered. There's no way around it—we often create monologues because we're more interested in ourselves than we are in the other person.

Years ago, one of my shift-mates wasn't even an assistant manager. I pointed out that I was very good at noticing scheduling issues.

He then recommended me to our manager as far as scheduling process improvements went. I later found out that he was actually doing this regularly regarding different ideas other people had. As a result, our unit was the most efficient and productive in the whole company. It was a fairly large company, so people started paying more attention to my shift-mate. It really did not surprise me to learn after several years that this person is now high up in the executive ranks of the company. He did not have a place in the hierarchy, but it was very clear that he cared about the interest of the company as a whole.

He wanted the company to succeed. That's

why he took it upon himself to figure out what everybody in his team was good at, and made management aware of what people could contribute. He enabled the team to build on its strengths and take its performance to the next level. He made everybody good around him because he recognized the mutual benefits.

Organic leaders take it upon themselves to make everybody shine around them. They don't shrink away when people express their brilliance. They don't feel threatened when people come up with great ideas. Instead, they look out for the welfare of the team—whether it is a work team, a friend group, or a baseball team. They think of the team as a whole. And by being the glue that holds people together, they rise along with everyone else.

Finally, organic leaders are proactive in seeking constructive feedback, even though it may be crouched in negative tones. They don't react emotionally. Instead, they focus on the substance and what they can take from it.

"Constructive" feedback is really a misnomer

because most "constructive" feedback is a rebuke or a slam. But if you are mature enough, you can phrase it in such a way that it can lead to constructive changes. Organic leaders know all about this. This is why they can pick up positive feedback that is often crouched in negative terms, and rephrase it to heighten the positive tone and pass it on. This then improves the atmosphere or operational processes of an organization.

"God, you are a terrible planner. I hated this weekend!"

It might sting for a second, but why did they have such a poor time? It's a strong reaction that warrants investigation if you can accept the feedback. By the same token, they proactively address questions and concerns and don't passively wait for them to come to them.

Listening to people and giving them an opportunity to vent their emotions is just an initial part of a larger process.

Organic leaders, on the other hand, proactively step into the shoes of other people and try to see the situation from their end. Once they have a fairly accurate perspective, they try to come up with a win-win situation. This is not always possible, but when it is, the results are dramatically superior.

You may not pick the people you work and spend most of your waking hours with, but that doesn't mean you can't turn them into friends, or at least allies, with the tactics in this chapter. You may be in an office, but people don't stop adhering to their interests or personalities once they step inside. Just remember that everyone is just like you and wants to feel valued, validated, and important. Taking that as a starting point might solve the majority of your issues immediately. After all, if you come across unpleasant people all day, it's likely that you are the unpleasant person in people's lives.

Conclusion

At this point, you might realize that you have far more toxic habits than you thought. If you feel self-conscious, that's not a bad thing, and it might even save you in the future.

You might not be a Dorothy (from the introduction of this book) per se, but it's the small nuances and details that really endear us to others and allow us to handle situations in just the right way. People can be so fickle that it's really worth it to arm ourselves as best as possible for whomever we come across.

You also might have realized that Dorothy was thinking solely in terms of her self-interests, not making any attempt at empathy, and creating a decidedly unsafe space for me to share—as in, I never wanted to share anything with her again. Not quite the effect we want.

Often, we can achieve exactly what we want in a situation or navigate it expertly just by taking a step back and acting as if other people are three-dimensional people.

Sincerely,

Patrick King
Social Interaction Specialist
www.PatrickKingConsulting.com

P.S. If you enjoyed this book, please don't be shy and drop me a line, leave a review, or both! I love reading feedback, and reviews are the lifeblood of Kindle books, so they are always welcome and greatly appreciated.

Speaking and Coaching

Imagine going far beyond the contents of this book and dramatically improving the way you interact with the world and the relationships you'll build.

Are you interested in contacting Patrick for the following?

- A social skills, active listening, or confrontation fluency workshop for your workplace
- Speaking engagements on the power of conversation and charisma
- Personalized social skills and conversation coaching

Patrick speaks around the world to help people improve their lives as a result of the power of building relationships with improved social skills. He is a recognized industry expert, bestselling author, and speaker.

To invite Patrick to speak at your next event or to inquire about coaching, get in touch directly through his website's contact form at http://www.PatrickKingConsulting.com/contact

Cheat Sheet

Chapter 1. Take Ownership and Responsibility

The first step to improving your people skills is to take responsibility for them. It's no one's duty but yours, and it influences how you view your life in general. It is all for you to proactively adjust, and you should not be waiting for it to come to you.

Chapter 2. Find Secondary Self-Interests

Once you understand people's primary and secondary self-interests, you understand them on a very deep level. The primary self-interest might be obvious, but the more covert self-interests might be more important.

Chapter 3. Reform Toxic Habits

Sometimes it's just as important to eliminate the negative as it is to improve the positive. We all possess toxic habits that may repel others, no matter how charming we are otherwise. For instance, being a conversational narcissist, not listening well, and a need to always be right.

Chapter 4. Question Your Assumptions

The assumptions we make about other people and the world in general are usually incorrect. Therefore, seek to poke holes in them and don't attribute malice prematurely.

Chapter 5. On Listening with Intent

We have two ears and only one mouth for a reason. We must learn to listen, and listen with intent. Listening is not a passive activity and allows others to take the spotlight.

Chapter 6. Emotional Intelligence

Emotional intelligence is the ability to understand your own emotions, and consequently, the emotions of people around you. This lets you understand their motivations on a deep level.

Chapter 7. Open the Door! Belief Police!

Sometimes we just feel the need to correct people. But what does it accomplish? The answer is almost always nothing. Let sleeping dogs lie and learn to let things go in favor of social lubrication.

Chapter 8. The Four Communication Styles

The four communication styles are passive, aggressive, passive-aggressive, and assertive. Assertive is the best balance where you can assert your needs but also cater to people as necessary.

Chapter 9. Walk a Mile

… in people's shoes. Only then will you know what they are truly feeling. This is the key to building empathy and is a process that makes you more people-centered.

Chapter 10. The Value of Shutting Up

We all need to shut up more. That little niggling thought in your mind – skip it. Stop it. Shut up. It doesn't accomplish anything and anyone that ever said whatever was on their mind was in reality a pompous blowhard.

Chapter 11. Connect Instantly

Connecting with people is a byproduct of people skills and can take many forms. If you try to care about others, banish the ulterior motives you have, practice, and learn to deal with negativity, you will have a leg up socially.

Chapter 12. Workplace Tactics

The office presents a unique set of challenges in regards to people skills. Chief among them are the need for tact and optics to better play office politics. Organic leadership, accountability, appreciation, and conflict management are among the challenges.

Printed in Great Britain
by Amazon